THE ROOT AND FRUIT OF ALL FAITH

The Deeper Truths and Understandings of the Bible

MICHAEL J HNATOWICZ III

Table of Contents

Introduction

Acknowledgment and Dedication Sermon

Chapter 1 The Father, Son, and Holy Spirit

Chapter 2 Baptism by Water and Fire

Chapter 3 God's Law of Love

Chapter 4 Under Law or Under Grace

Chapter 5 Faith that Produces Good Fruit

Chapter 6 Shadow of Things to Come

Chapter 7 Unity through Separation

Chapter 8 Pairs by Equal Opposites

Chapter 9 The Natural and Spiritual

Chapter 10 The Battle Between Spirit and Flesh

Chapter 11 Fallen Angels and Idol gods

Chapter 12 Eternal Life After Death

Conclusion

Introduction

I gained a deeper truth and understanding to the Bible. I understand that the Bible teaches me how to live. I live each day trying to produce good fruit and to share God's Word.

This is the reason I began to write this book.

To share with a larger audience the things of my understanding. To share with you the deeper truths and understandings of the Bible. To be rooted and grounded in faith and in love and to produce good fruit.

Acknowledgment and Dedication

"GOD IS CALLING US"

God is calling us to be his sheep, sons and daughters of God, men and women of God, servants of God, vessels of God, who walk in Spirit and are filled with spirit. Doers of the word not just hearers of the word.

Who seek to do the will of God and to follow in his ways, which his ways are righteousness. God is righteousness, truth, and justice. God is fair, just, and true. We should want to be like our Father.

Seeking to do his will. Striving to do good, eager to speak the truth, quick to forgive, loving and correcting each other in righteousness and kindness. Leading each other out of darkness and leading those to Christ, who is the light that leads men from their sinful ways.

The whole Bible can be summed up in the idea that there is good and evil, righteousness and wickedness, and that God punishes the wicked and rewards the righteous, that He despises what is evil and loves what is good.

God is calling us to be bold and to be set apart from the world. To be in the world but not of the world. To not follow the ways of the world but to follow the ways of God. The works of righteousness and faith. To stand upright and firm in righteousness and goodness. And to be planted and grounded in love and faith.

Throughout the Bible from the garden of Eden, Cain and Abel, Noah and the Flood, Sodom and Gomorrah, we see a common theme. That God destroys the wicked and saves the righteous. That He despises the evil and rewards the good.

He is telling us to flee from sin, flee from temptation, flee from evil. Just like Babylon he is calling us to come out of her, to come out of sin, to come out of our wicked ways. God is calling out to us like John the Baptist in the wilderness saying: ye all repent and be baptized for the kingdom of God is at hand.

To turn back to God and set our faith in him. To be baptized in the name of the Father, the Son, and the Holy Spirit. To be baptized in the name of Jesus Christ. To have faith in the complete work of Christ Jesus.

God counts our faith alone as righteousness and rewards our good deeds. It is by faith that you are saved and this is not by your own works but by the Grace of God.

God is a God of faith and just as Abraham was faithful and he believed and it was accounted to him as righteousness. Our faith in Christ Jesus is accounted to us as righteousness.

Christ is made for us our righteousness and God is our Justification. He is Grace, Mercy, and Love. He is Justifier and Redeemer. In our weakness He is made strong. In my weakness He is my strength.

We are called to preach his word and to be a vessel for God. That we plant good seeds, good words, and good deeds. That we have faith that produces good fruit.

He is calling us to be the good tree that bears good fruit. The fruit of the Spirit. For every tree that doesn't bear good fruit will be cut down. He is calling us to be rooted and grounded in faith and in love. God is calling us to lead and live a life of integrity and morals.

God is calling us to have faith, faith in His only begotten Son, to be the good and faithful servant, vessels of God doing the will of God. God is a God of faith and is calling us to have complete faith in Him and in His Son.

To have the faith of a mustard seed, to believe on His Son who shed his blood for your sins, who died, was buried, and resurrected. Ascended into Heaven, seated at the Right Hand of God, and will come again in his Glory.

To have faith in the work Christ did and faith in His saving blood. Faith in the resurrection and the Second Coming of Christ Jesus. Faith that God will never abandon nor forsake you. That God is Justifier and Redeemer and it is by faith and grace that we are saved.

God is calling us to receive His Holy Spirit. To pray and ask, believe and receive, the Holy Spirit. To be Sealed by the Holy Spirit. To be filled with Spirit and to walk in Spirit.

Saved by Grace through Faith by the Love of God. For God so loved the world that He gave His only begotten Son so that whosoever believe in Him shall not perish but have everlasting life.

CHAPTER 1

The Father Son and Holy Spirit

Who is the Father? Who is the Son? Who is the Holy Spirit? And how are these three made One?

Is God all three in one making up One God? Or is there One God alone that has three distinct persons that are equal? Is there a hierarchy or an order to their persons?

I want to look deeper into this discussion because there are many different perspectives that slightly differ from one denomination to the other.

Things like is God Jesus and is Jesus God? Is the Son literally taking place of the Father?

Did Jesus see himself as greater or equal to God the Father, or do they share a relationship with each other?

Did God the Father come down from heaven, or did He send His Son down for us?

I believe there is God the Father, the one and only true God. He has His one and only begotten Son, who is the Son of God.

There is the Holy Spirit, which is the Spirit of God, and proceeds from the Father and is shared with His Son.

They are three distinct persons that are One in likeness and Holiness, equal in Power, Honor, and Glory in the order of Father, Son, and Holy Spirit.

I will go into each of these persons and their position to clearly see the mystery and relationship between the Father, the Son, and Holy Spirit.

God the Father, Almighty God, Our Father, Creator of Heaven and Earth, The Most High, the One and Only True God who Created all things. These are some the titles of God the Father.

God is a Spirit, He is Eternal and Self-existent, having no beginning or no end. He is Holy, Righteous, and True. God is One and He alone is God. He is the source of all life and creation.

He is Father over all creation and Father of His one and only begotten Son. Why is He called Father? Let us think about it, what do we know about an earthly father?

The father is the head of the house, a father is a giver of life, bearing a seed. The father sets the rules or gives the law. The father loves and corrects his children.

In the same way we understand a father's love for his children, we can understand how God the Father loves us and His Son.

God the Father loves his Son, He would want to give all that He has to His Son, He would want His Son to be honored. He gives His Son for us so that we may be reconciled to God as His Children.

John 3:35 "The Father love the Son and have given all things into his hand."

John 5:23 "That all men should honor the Son, even as they honor the Father. He that honor not the Son honor not the Father which have sent Him."

Therefore, we call God Father because He is Life and He is Father over all creation. We all come from Our Father for we were created by God.

Malachi 2:10 "Have we not all one Father? Has not one God created us?"

1 Corinthians 8:6 "Yet for us there is one God, the Father, from whom are all things and for whom we exist, and one Lord, Jesus Christ, through whom are all things and through whom we exist."

Ephesians 4:6 "One God and Father of all, who is over all and through all and in all."

The Father is sovereign over all things for He is the source of all Creation. He is through all things for all things were Created through His Son, the Word of God. He is in all things by Creation and through His Holy Spirit.

He is Father of His only begotten Son, begotten not made, in which, the Son not being created by God but coming directly from God.

The Father works through His Son, and the Son being just like His Father does the will of His Father.

Like the saying goes "Like Father like Son."

John 5:19-20 Then Jesus answered and said unto them, Verily, Verily I say unto you, the Son can do nothing of himself, but what he sees the Father do, for what things so ever He do, these also the Son do likewise."

The Son of God, the Word of God, the Lamb of God who takes away the sins of the world. The only begotten Son of the Father, who was in the beginning with God, who all things created were created through Him by Him and for Him.

John 1:1-3 "In the beginning was the Word, and the Word was with God, and the Word was God. The same was in the beginning with God. All things were made by him and without him was not anything made that was made."

The Word became flesh coming down from Heaven to reconcile us back to the Father. The Son is Holy, Eternal, Righteous, and True. He is honored and glorified by the Father, that in Him the Father is glorified.

John 1:14 "And the Word became flesh and dwelt among us, and we have seen his glory, glory as of the Only Son from the Father, full of Grace and Truth."

The Son is perfectly just like his Father, bearing the image of His Father, and being one with the Father. But does that make him the Father?

Let us think of it this way. You have an earthly father and you are the son. You come from your father, but you are not your daddy.

The Father and the Son are two distinct persons but are alike and are one because the Son comes from his Father. The son looks just like his father, acts like his father, loves and honors his father, is exactly like his father but does not take the place of his father.

In the same manner, God is the Father and Christ is His Son. The Son is just like His Father doing the will of the Father. Aiming to please his Father and to be obedient to the Father. This is bearing His image and being one with the Father.

The Son loves and honors His Father and is exactly like His Father but does not take the place of the Father. The Father also loves and honors His Son and is pleased with His Son.

John 5:30 "I can of my own self do nothing: as I hear, I judge and my judgment is Just; because I seek not my own will, but the Will of the Father which have sent me."

John 6:38 "For I came down from heaven, not to do mine own will, but the Will of Him that sent me."

John 14:31 "But the world may know that I Love the Father, and as the Father gave me commandment, even so I do."

The Father is well pleased with His Son and like a Good Father wants to give all to His Son. For this reason, God gives His Son Glory by having all life renewed through Him. The Father loves the Son and gives Him all things.

John 1:4 "In him was Life, and the life was the light of men."

John 5:26 "For as the Father have life in himself, so have he given to the Son to have Life in himself."

John 12:28 "Father glorify thy name. Then came there a voice from heaven saying, "I have both glorified it, and will glorify it again."

How did the Son view his relationship with the Father? Was he saying that He is God the Father in the flesh? Or that when you see the Son you have seen the Father because the Father is in Him? Did God come down from heaven or did He send His Son down for us?

The bible says that God is a Spirit and His throne is in the Highest Heavens. That He sent His one and only Son, the Word of God, who was in the beginning with God, the Son of God who came down from heaven, born in the flesh, to die for our sins so that we may be reconciled through His death and resurrection.

After His death and resurrection, He ascended back into heaven and is seated at the right hand of the Father.

Hebrews 1:3 "He is the radiance of the Glory of God and the exact imprint of his nature, and he upholds the universe by the word of his power. After making purification for sins, he sat down at the right hand of the Majesty on High,"

So, let us examine this further.

The Father and Son must be two persons. First, because the Father sends the Son and that Jesus constantly emphasizes, He was sent by God saying, "it is He who sent me"

John 17:3 "And this is eternal life, that they know you the only true God, and Jesus Christ whom you have sent."

Second, the Father was in Heaven when the Son prayed to Him on earth. He could not be praying to himself but instead was praying to His Father and Our Father.

Third, to be seated at the right hand of the Father signifies that there are two positions, one being God the Father and one being the Son who is seated at His right hand.

Not only that but just having the distinct roles of Father and Son shows that there are two positions and a relationship shared between the two.

Let us look at some scriptures where the Son explains his relationship with the Father and how he is one with his Father.

John 8:29 "And He that sent me is with me; the Father have not left me alone; for I do always those things that Please him."

John 10:30 "I and my Father are one."

John 12:49 "For I have not spoken of myself, but the Father which sent me, he gave me a commandment, what I should say and what I should speak."

John 10:29 "My Father, which gave them me, is greater than all; and no man is able to pluck them out of my Fathers hand."

John 12:44 "Jesus cried and said, He that believe on me, believe not on me, but on him that sent me."

John 13:20 "Verily, Verily I say unto you, He that receive whomsoever I send receive me, and he that receive me receive him that sent me."

We see here that the Father is with Jesus through the Holy Spirit. He says the Father has not left me alone and that I and my Father are one. The Holy Spirit is the Spirit of God and Christ having the Holy Spirit makes him one with God.

With Gods presence he was not alone and <u>by</u> being on one accord with the Father through the Spirit, He spoke the things God would speak and does the Will of His Father.

He also says, "He that believes on me believes in the One who sent me", which explains how the Son viewed his relationship with the Father. He gives ~~The~~the Father Glory, Honor, and Praise, and tells us to worship the Father, who is greater than all.

One Scripture reads, "I and the Father are One" which describes their divine nature and essence. Another reads "The Father is Greater than I" which describes their position and headship.

To understand this relationship, we must take both scriptures into context. Jesus is the one and only Son of the one and only True God.

Christ says, "I and the Father are One" but he does not say "I am the Father." We do not say "The Son is the Father" but we can say "The Son and the Father are One, in relation to the Holy Spirit." There is an order of authority, hierarchy, and headship.

1 Corinthians 11:3 But I want you to realize that the head of every man is Christ, and the head of woman is man, and the head of Christ is God."

The Father is the Head, yet this does not take away from the divinity of the Son and Holy Spirit. The Son constantly receives His glory, power, throne, and honor from the Father and lives to glorify the Father.

As well the Spirit lives to glorify the Father and the Son. God is One but it does not say Three in One. The One true God is the Father and His only begotten Son is the Son of God. The Holy Spirit is the Spirit of God, whereby, these three are One in likeness and Holiness in fullness.

Colossians 2:9 "For in him the whole fullness of deity dwells bodily,"

1 John 5:7 "For there are three that bear record in heaven, the Father, the Word, and the Holy Spirit: and these three are one."

These three are One in the Father and are One in likeness to the Father. Through His Holy Spirit, Christ is One with God and through the Holy Spirit we are made One in Christ, who is One with God. This is how we become Children of the Most High through His Son and His Spirit by becoming like Christ and more like our Father.

Galatians 3:26-29 "So in Christ Jesus you are all children of God through faith, for all of you were baptized into Christ have clothed yourselves with Christ.

Romans 8:10-16 However, if Christ lives in you, your bodies are dead because of sin, but your spirits are alive because you have God's approval. Does the Spirit of the one who brought Jesus back to life live in you? Then the one who brought Christ back to life will also make your mortal bodies alive by his Spirit who lives in you. Certainly, all who are guided by God's Spirit are God's Children. the Spirit himself testifies with our spirit that we are God's children."

The Son is in us by His Spirit, God the Father is in us by His Spirit, the same Spirit, but again Jesus is not the Father. Although the fullness of God the Father is expressed bodily in his Son. God revealed himself to us through his Son, that He is the image of God and the Word of God, being the physical representation of who the Father is spiritually and speaking the things the Father would speak. Who better to send than His Son? Whom is exactly like his Father doing the Will of his Father.

John 14:20 *"At that day you shall know that I am in the Father, and you in me, and I in you."*

    The Holy Spirit, The Spirit of God, the Spirit of Life which proceeds from the Father and shared with his Son. The Spirit of God is Holy, Eternal, Righteous, and True. Being the true essence of the Father by having all the attributes of the Father. Who was left for us as a mighty counselor and guide in wisdom. The Spirit that dwells with God in His dwelling place coming known to us through His Son.

When we receive and are transformed by the Holy Spirit, we become One with Christ, which is One with God. It is through his Holy Spirit we are made into One body by One Spirit on One accord.

The Bible says "There are three that bear witness in Heaven, which is the Father, the Son, and the Holy Spirit. In the beginning the Word was with God and the Holy Spirit which proceeds from God.

Genesis 1 states that "the Spirit of God came down on the surfaces of the deep" showing that the Spirit of God was there in the beginning.

Also, in Genesis we recall the well-known scripture "let US make man in OUR image and in OUR likeness" notice the emphasis on the word "US" and "OUR" stating that these three are one in likeness but are three distinct persons. If not so, it would read "I created man in my image" right?

God the Father, the Word of God, and the Spirit of God were all active in Creation. Remember it says that all things were Created through him by him and for him. That the Father Created all things through His Son, for His Son, by His Son, through the power of the Holy Spirit.

Colossians 1:16 "For by him all things were created, in heaven and on earth, visible and invisible, whether thrones or dominions or ruler or authorities-all things were created through him and for him."

It is by the Will of God that the Word speaks it and the Spirit brings it into existence. God the Father Wills it, The Word of God speaks it, and the Spirit fulfills the Word.

Scripture says, "God's word goes out and will not come back void." What does this mean? If God Wills it, then it surely will come to pass.

For example, the scripture "let there be light" and "there was light". Let me explain, it is by the Fathers Will that there be light, the Word spoke the Will of the Father, hence the Word of God.

He spoke "Let there be Light" and the Spirt goes out and fulfills the Word of God, not coming back void but manifesting the Will of God and Word of God, which is seen when it says "and there was light".

Then the Father saw what was created and saw that it was Good. So now we can see how all things were Created from God, through His Word, and by the Holy Spirit.

We see how the Son and Spirit come directly from the Father, how they were in the beginning together before creation, and how they are one in likeness and Holiness being in the image of God.

The Father is Holy, The Son is Holy, and the Spirit is Holy, as the scripture reads "Holy, Holy, Holy" these three are One and we can see how the Son is One with his Father because they share the same Holy Spirit.

How are these three made one? Do we take this literally or figuratively? Is it three that make up One God? Or is it One God, His Son, and His Holy Spirit who are one in likeness and essence?

Let us look at a scripture, *1 Corinthians 10:17 "Because there is One loaf, we who are many, are one body, for we all share the One loaf."*

Here Christ shows us another idea of how many parts are all part of the whole. Think of slices of bread that come from a loaf. Although there are many slices, they still all come from the one loaf, and are one with the loaf even if broken off into slices.

Now think about it this way, God the Father represents the One loaf or One God. The parts that come from the loaf, the first and second slice, would be the Son and the

Spirit. Although there are three equal parts or persons, they all come from the whole or the one loaf, or One God. By extending this out to us who believe in His Son and by receiving His Holy Spirit, we become One with Christ as the body of Christ, which are members or parts of a whole.

We are One in Christ, with One Spirit, One body, One mind, and on One accord, whereby, we become One with the Son, who is One with the Father.

———————

Therefore, the Son always glorifies the Father and says, "I and the Father are One, I come from my Father, The Father is in me, and I am in the Father." Christ is saying, He and the Father are One because he came from his Father and the Spirit that proceeds from the Father is one with the Son.

The Son is just like His Father and His Spirit is the very spirit and essence of God, for it is Gods Spirit. The Spirit is all that He is and the Son who shares the same Spirit is just like His Father, therefore, perfectly making them all one in likeness and Holiness.

They come from the One God, the Father, not coming together to make up three Gods in One, instead they together are One with the Father having come from the Father.

In the same manner, we who are one with Christ become the Body of Christ, whereby we are many parts of a whole, many members to One Body. Although we are many members or parts of the whole, we are considered as one with the whole. Whereby, we are one in Christ, who is the head of the body, and we understand that God is the Head of Christ.

This means that through Christ and by the Holy Spirit, we become children of God, sons and daughters of the Most High, who live in accordance with God's Will, being made one with Christ and the Father.

1 Corinthians 12:12-14 "Just as a body, though one, has many parts, but all its many parts form one body, so it is with Christ. For we were all baptized by one Spirit to form one body--whether Jews or Gentiles, slave or free--and we were all given the one Spirit to drink. Even so the body is not made up of one part but of many."

This helps us better understand how three are made one or how many members are part of a whole. To understand that God is One and is the whole and His Word and Spirit both extend from Him. To understand the Father as being, the Source of all things, the One, and Almighty God the Father. That all goodness comes from God. That God is One and He alone is God, that His Son is the One and Only begotten Son of God, and that the Holy Spirit is the One Spirit of God.

Another way to look at it is to think about the Three Musketeers. For example, their famous saying was what? "One for All and All for One" What does this mean? Are the three musketeers combined into one musketeer?

Or are there three musketeers who are on one accord, one mind, one spirit, with one goal. By this they were all for the same cause and stood for the same things, we could say they was on one accord.

They were all for the One and the One was for the all. This what makes three into one literally and figuratively. The Son and the Spirit literally come from the Father, however, figuratively they are One in likeness and divinity and holiness.

What makes them equal? They are one in likeness and in divine nature by sharing the attributes of the Father. The Father is Divine, Holy, and Eternal, whereby, the Son and the Holy Spirit coming from the Father are Divine, Holy, and Eternal.

They were all present in the beginning of Creation. The Father being the Will of God, the Son the Word of God, and the Holy Spirit the Spirit of God. The Father Wills it, the Son speaks it, the Spirit fulfills it. All things were Created by the Will of God, through the Word of God, and by the power of His Holy Spirit.

Therefore, this makes them co-creators, co-eternal, and co- existent upon the Father. The Father has Life, Power, Honor, and Glory in Him. The Father also gives Life, Power, Honor, and Glory to His Son. The Holy Spirit is left to us having Life, Power, Honor, and Glory.

The Spirit glorifies the Father and the Son, the Son glorifies His Father, and the Father receiving all Glory gives honor to his Son and His Spirit, which are one with the Father.

We see that they are equal or one in likeness and Holiness, having Power, Honor, and Glory. However, they are three distinct persons that are not One God, but are on one accord, one Spirit, and are one mind with the Father.

All being parts of the whole, not equally divided so that the Father is third parts of the whole, but that the Father is the whole from which all parts are one with.

Now we see who each one is and their relationship with each other, and how they are equal or one in likeness by having the same one Spirit. They do not come together as One or a Godhead, but together they are one with the Father.

My question is, in this Godhead is there an order or a hierarchy? Does this Godhead combine to make this One God, or is the Father the One God and from Him comes the Son of God and the Spirit of God?

Is it God the Father, God the Son, God the Holy Spirit? This can be misleading or confusing to some because it eludes that Three Gods make up this One Triune God, a trinitarian God.

More clearly stated would be God the Father, the Son of God, and the Spirit of God. This shows clearly that there is

One God the Father and from Him comes His Son and Spirit who are one with the Father. These three are not made into One God but that they are one with this One God, the Father.

The trinity is described in the Godhead saying that the Godhead or Trinity becomes this One God. In contrast, the One God is the Father and is the head, not the Godhead itself. If there is this Godhead of Father, Son, and Holy Spirit, then the Father is the head not making all three into one.

Headship shows that there is not only an order but a hierarchy that goes from Father, Son, and Holy Spirit. With the Father as the Head of Christ, and Christ as the head of man, in which, the Spirit leads us to the Son who leads us to the Father, who is the head of us all.

We can see that they are equal in likeness and Holiness, that they are one with the Father, and that the Father is the Head and not the Godhead itself.

1 Corinthians 11:3 "But I would have you know, that the head of every man is Christ, and the head of woman is the man, and the head of Christ is God."

Luke 4:8 Jesus answered, "It is written: 'Worship the Lord your God and serve him only." 17 Jesus said to her "Stop clinging to me, for I have not yet ascended to the Father, but go to my brothers and say unto them, 'I ascend to my Father and your Father, and my God and your God."

Let us investigate this some more. Who comes first, a Father or Son? Who is the head of the house? Although they are one household the Father is the head of the house.

John 13:16 "Verily, Verily I say unto you. The servant is not greater than his Lord, neither he that is sent greater than he that sent him."

John 14:30 "If you loved me you would rejoice, because I said I go unto the Father; for my Father is Greater than I."

Even in the Godhead trinity, the Father would remain the Head, so that we see there is an order with "God First" even as the Son told us in the first commandment, which is to love God with all your heart, mind, and soul.

On the other hand, the Father tells us to honor His Son, that the Father has given the Son all that the Father has. The Father gives all Power, Honor, and Glory to His Son and the Son lives to glorify his Father.

We can see they honor each other, and we see a clear relationship between the Father and Son and their positions. The position of Father and Son, the Father with His Throne and His Son who is seated at his right hand with his Throne.

Christ says, "The Father is greater than I". Was this only in his physical perspective or was it a clear message that the Son comes from his Father, that he is one with His Father, and that the Father is over him?

This would show a headship or hierarchy that leads us back to the Father through His Son by His Spirit.

Just as the Father, the Son has received Life, Power, Honor, and Glory from his Father and in His glory, he glorifies the Father. In us the Spirit glorifies the Son, in which, in Him we give all Glory back to God the Father.

So, we see that they are three distinct persons, equal or one in divine nature and essence, coming directly from the Father, having been given Power, Honor, and Glory from the Father, and in the order of Father, Son, and Holy Spirit.

One source stated, "All things-the entire created realm, both physical and spiritual- is ultimately from God the Father, it was all made through His Son. And His Son rules over all creation as Lord and King under the Father.

1 Corinthians 15:24 "Then the end will come, when he hands over the kingdom to God the Father after he has destroyed all dominion, authority and power. For he must reign until he has put all his enemies under his feet. The last enemy to be destroyed is death. For he "has put everything under his feet. Now when it says that 'everything" has been put under him, it is clear that this does not include God himself, who put everything under Christ. When he has done this, then the Son himself will be made subject to him who put everything under him, so that God may be all in all.

In Conclusion, we see that there are three distinct persons, the Father, the Son, and Holy Spirit and that these three and are one in likeness and Holiness.

That there is an order and hierarchy that goes from Father to Son, in which, they are equal by sharing the same Spirit of God.

We see that the Father gives what he has to His Son, all life, power, honor, and glory and that the Son gives all power, honor, and glory back to the Father.

They are One by One Spirit with a position of Father and Son. That the Son sits at the right hand of the Father, the Father is before the Son, and the Father is over the Son, but like a good Father has given all things to His Son.

"So as there is life in the Father, so now there is life in the Son." We see the Son has life in him and is to be honored just as the Father. *"If you honor me then you honor my Father who sent me."*

The Spirit of God, being the very essence of God, who is everything God is, is to be honored just as the Father. Therefore, these three are Holy, Holy, Holy and are One with the Father, not as One God, but as three equal persons in likeness and in the order of Father, Son, and Holy Spirit.

The One God, the Father, is the head and His Son and Spirit are part of the whole. When they come together, they are One with the Father, who is God. Whereby, through His Son and His Spirit we become one with the Father, therefore, becoming Children of the Most High God.

Chapter 2

Baptism by Water and by Fire

What does it mean to be baptized? What does it mean to be baptized by water and by fire? What is the significance of each and how do they together represent baptism?

The word baptize means to submerge or immerse. When a person is baptized, they are submerged or immersed in water as a pledge of allegiance, a proclamation of faith, and a belief in Jesus Christ and in His death, burial, and resurrection. Water baptism is a Profession of Faith, where a person proclaims their belief in the Father, the Son, and the Holy Spirit. It is an outward public display of one's discipleship and new life in Christ.

1 Peter 3:21 "And this water symbolizes baptism that now saves you also--not the removal of dirt from the body but the pledge of a clear conscience toward God. It saves you by the resurrection of Jesus Christ."

The baptism represents the death, burial, and resurrection of Jesus Christ and how we have died with Christ and now live in Christ.

Romans 6:4 "We were therefore buried with him through baptism into death in order that, just as Christ was raised from the dead through the glory of the Father, we too may live a new life."

We go under the water and put to death the old self and we come up from the water into a new life in Christ.

Colossians 3:9-10 "Do not lie to each other, since you have taken off your old self with its practices and have put on the new self, which is being renewed in knowledge in the image of its Creator."

The water represents life, renewal, and rebirth. It also represents the pouring out of the spirit and the cleansing and washing away of our sins. Water is a symbol for life, renewal, and rebirth and described as water everlasting, rivers of living water, or the fountain of life. In the Bible, water is usually attributed as drinking from the fountain or cup of everlasting life, a replenishing, refreshing, and eternal source of life. It is also represented as water that cleanses and washes away; making us clean. It helps us to understand how the spirit was poured out for us and how it cleanses and washes away our sins, giving us eternal life, renewal, and rebirth. Here are some examples of how water is used symbolically for the Spirit.

John 7:37 "Now on the last day, the great day of the feast, Jesus stood and cried out saying, "If anyone is thirsty, let him come to me and drink, "He who believes in me, as the Scripture said, from his innermost being will flow rivers of living water." But this He spoke of the Spirit, whom those who believe in Him were to receive."

Isaiah 44:3 "For I will pour out water on the thirsty land and streams on the dry ground; I will pour out My Spirit on your offspring and My blessing on your descendants."

John 4:14 but whoever drinks of the water that I will give him shall never thirst; but the water that I will give him will become in him a well of water springing up to eternal life."

The first example of water baptism is John the Baptist, in which, he baptized by water for the repentance and forgiveness of sins. He explained that One would come after him that will baptize by fire with the Holy Spirit and for salvation and redemption from sin.

Matthew 3:11 "I baptize you with water for repentance. But after me comes one who is more powerful than I, whose sandals I am not worthy to carry. He will baptize you with the Holy Spirit and fire."

Luke 3:3 "And he came into all the district around the Jordan, preaching a baptism of repentance for the forgiveness of sins."

Mark 1:4-5 "John the Baptist appeared in the wilderness preaching a baptism of repentance for the forgiveness of sins. And all the country of Judea was going out to him; and all the people of Jerusalem; and they were baptized by him in the Jordan river, confessing their sins."

John was to prepare the way for the Lord and the water baptism was to precede Christ baptism. In other words, the water baptism prepares us for the receiving of the Holy Spirit.

Matthew 3:3 "This is he who was spoken of through the prophet Isaiah: A voice of one calling in the wilderness, "Prepare the way for the Lord, make straight paths for him."

This represents how the water baptism of John was to prepare us and help us better understand the Spirit and what was to come. Water baptism not only pledges your allegiance to God and professes your faith in Christ as his disciple but helps us understand symbolically how water or the Spirit cleanses and washes away our sins.

1 Peter 3:21 "And this water symbolizes baptism that now saves you also--not the removal of dirt from the body but the pledge of a clear conscience toward God. It saves you by the resurrection of Jesus Christ."

The symbolism here shows that not only does water symbolically wash away dirt but metaphorically is speaking of the Spirit that washes away sin.

The water baptism is a symbol of faith and preparation for the receiving of the Holy Spirit, which is, the baptism by fire.

When we are baptized, we profess our faith in Jesus and we confess and repent of our sins, and we believe and partake in the death and resurrection of Christ through baptism by water.

Water baptism precedes the fire baptism because it prepares us and helps us understand the receiving of the Holy Spirit.

Water baptism should lead to the praying for the Holy Spirit and baptism by fire, which is, the receiving of the

Holy Spirit. Spirit baptism is the reality and manifestation of the symbolic water baptism.

The water is symbolic of the Spirit and fire is symbolic of the Spirit, the fire is set apart from the water to distinguish between the two, which is, John's baptism by water and Christ's baptism by fire.

We see these as two progressive acts in that you are baptized by water through immersion and baptized by Spirit by praying for the Holy Spirit and being filled with the Holy Spirit.

In the bible, we see disciples of Jesus laying hands on believers who were baptized, and they received the Holy Spirit.

Acts 8:12 "But when they believed Philip as he proclaimed the good news of the kingdom of God and the name of Jesus Christ, they were baptized, both man and women. 14 When the Apostles in Jerusalem heard that Samaria had accepted the word of God, they sent Peter and John to Samaria. 15 When they arrived, they prayed for the new believers there that they might receive the Holy Spirit, 16 because the Holy Spirit had not yet come on any of them, they had simply been baptized in the name of the Lord Jesus. 17 then Peter and John placed their hands on them, and they received the Holy Spirit." As we see new believers that accepted the word of God were baptized by water in the name of Jesus Christ before they received the Holy Spirit. The Apostles did not lay their hands on them until they had already proclaimed their belief in Christ through baptism. Baptism by water is represented by the immersion into water and our profession of faith, however, the Spirit baptism is represented by the laying of hands and praying for the Holy Spirit. Receiving the Holy Spirit is the Gift that Jesus promised He would leave as a comforter and was the Spirit He was speaking of through baptism by fire.

Acts 1:4 "On one occasion, while he was eating with them, he gave them this command: "Do not leave Jerusalem, but wait for the gift my Father promised, which you have heard me speak about. 5 For John baptized with water, but in a few days, you will be baptized with the Holy Spirit." We see John's baptism is represented by water and Christ's baptism is represented by fire, in which, I believe is to differentiate between the two. The Apostles were told to wait in Jerusalem for the Holy Spirit, the gift of which he spoke about. The Apostles on the day of Pentecost received the Holy Spirit and were filled up with the indwelling Spirit of God.

Romans 8:9 "The Holy Spirit is the presence of God as He indwells the heart of the believer." They prayed and sang songs of praise and hymns and they were filled with the Holy Spirit.

Acts 2:1-4 "When the day of Pentecost came, they were all together in one place in one accord. Suddenly a sound like the blowing of a violent wind came from heaven and filled the whole house where they were sitting. They saw what seemed to be tongues of fire that separated and came to rest on each of them. All of them were filled with the Holy Spirit."

These Apostles were already believers in Christ, and witnessing in His resurrection and proclaiming His name, then they received the Holy Spirit.

When we receive the Holy Spirit it truly cleanses us and washes away our sins and allows us to be forgiven and to live fully in Christ through the Spirit.

Acts 2:38 "Peter replied "Repent and be baptized, every one of you, in the name of Jesus Christ for the forgiveness of sins. And you will receive the gift of the Holy Spirit. The promise is for you and your children and for all who are far off--for all whom the Lord our God will call."

We see that we are to be baptized by water in the name of Jesus for forgiveness of sins, in which, we will receive the gift and promise of the Holy Spirit that He spoke of, which is represented as the baptism of Spirit by fire. The Spirit is represented by fire to differentiate from the water baptism, but also, because the Spirit is like that of fire. In the same way we are immersed in water, we are consumed in fire.

Fire represents spirit, life, renewal, and rebirth, in which, it also represents the purification and refining process of the soul.

In some cultures, the phoenix bird is described as a fire bird that represents rebirth, renewal, immortality, resurrection, and transformation. It is said that early Christians liked the idea of the Phoenix because of its characteristics and similarity to the Spirit.

The Spirit is understood in the same manner that it represents rebirth, renewal, eternal life, resurrection, and transformation. The Spirit is also referenced in the bible as having characteristics of fire. How is the Holy Spirit like fire?

Fire can be used to illuminate or reveal things in the dark, used to purify and refine, and is seen as a source of light. The Spirit reveals truth, purifies and cleanses, and is a light in the dark. The Spirit is described symbolically with fire as God's presence, power, and purity.

The Bible describes God as a consuming fire and is often used as symbol of God's presence like the burning bush of Moses. Fire also is a symbol of Gods judgement and sign of His power and Spirit. The spirit is described in *Romans 12:1 "engulfed by the divine gift: the inextinguishable fire of the Holy Spirit."* The Spirit is described as a fire that engulfs and is inextinguishable. Being engulfed means that the Spirit consumes you and sets you on fire for God, creating a passion and love for God that is inextinguishable and will never go out, whereby, we have an eternal love for God and have everlasting life through the Spirit. The Spirit burns inside of us like a consuming fire, the disciples described their hearts as "burning within us" after talking with Jesus. This fire is not a natural fire but a spiritual fire symbolic for the Holy Spirit. For example, in *Exodus 3:2 "the angel of the Lord appeared to him in a flame of fire out of the midst of a bush. He looked, and behold, the bush was burning, yet it was not consumed"* Here we see that the fire is not a natural fire that consumes literally but a spiritual fire that metaphorically consumes our hearts. God's fire does not hurt his children--it cleanses, purifies, and frees our spirits, minds, and hearts.

God reveals things to us through His Spirit. Just as fire reveals and illuminates, the Spirit reveals things to us and illuminates us with the truth. Here are some examples of how fire is used as the spirit.

1 Corinthians 3:13 *"their work will be shown for what it is, because the day will bring it to light. It will be revealed with fire, and the fire will test the quality of each person's work."*

Here the fire is represented as the Spirit that will test and reveal each person's works and character. It can be read as, "It will be revealed with Spirit, and the Spirit will test the quality of each one's work."

Fire is also used is in the purification of gold where it refines and removes any impurities in the gold. Fire is represented as the Spirit that purifies and removes impurities within our self. We are represented by gold and the Spirit by fire. The fire is something that test us and refines us and removes any imperfections in us sanctifying us through a purification process. We see that the Spirit alike test our faith and character by convicting us and compelling us to remove any impurities by refining us, this represents the purification and sanctification of the Spirit.

One source wrote, The Holy Spirit produces the purity of God in our lives. God's purpose is to purify us, and the Spirit is the agent of our sanctification. As the silversmith uses fire to purge the dross from the precious metal, so God uses the Spirit to remove our sin from us.

Here are a few scriptures that describe fire and the refining process.

Zechariah 13:9 And I will put this third into the fire, and refine them as one refines silver, and test them as gold is tested.

Isaiah 48:10 Behold, I have refined you, but not as silver; I have tried you in the furnace of affliction.

Job 23:10 "But he knows the way I take; when he has tried me, I shall come out as gold."

Psalms 66:10 For you, O God, have tested us; you have tried us as silver is tried.

Proverbs 17:3 The crucible is for silver, and the furnace is for gold, and the Lord test hearts."

1 Peter 4:12 Beloved, do not be surprised at the fiery trial when it comes upon you to test you, as though something strange were happening to you.

1 Peter 1:7 So that the tested genuineness of your faith-- more precious than gold that perishes though it is tested by fire--may be found to result in praise and glory and honor at the revelation of Jesus Christ."

These examples describe how God test us like gold is tested with fire to purify, cleanse, and refine us to pure gold. Although we can understand the process of refining gold, it is only used symbolically to help us understand Spirit.

The Spirit is testing us like fire and purging away any impurities in us. For example, we may have impure feelings of hate, jealousy, pride, envy, and greed in our hearts which need to be purged and removed.

Mark 7:21 *"For it is from within, out of a person's heart, that evil thoughts come--sexual immorality, theft, murder, adultery, greed, malice, deceit, lust, envy, slander, pride, arrogance and foolishness. All these evils come from within and defile a person."*

These are evil thoughts that come from within and defile a person, however, it is through the Spirit that we purge and remove these impurities within us.

Think of it this way, the furnace is the trials of life and the things we go thru in life, which are hard times and the things that test our patience and kindness.

These are things that humble us and teach us the lessons in life. These trials in life are supposed to test us and refine us over time.

The Spirit is what purges and removes all the imperfections and refines you into the ways of the Spirit, showing you how to love, be humble, modest, patient, good and kind, therefore, purging away the old self and being refined in the Spirit.

Galatians 5:22 But the fruit of the Spirit is love, joy, peace, patience, kindness, goodness, faithfulness, meekness and self-control. Against such things there is no law."

We can see that both water and fire represent renewal, rebirth, cleansing and purifying, a removal of old self and the transformation of the new self.

The water helps us to understand how we are cleansed and made clean and fire helps us understand how we are refined and made pure.

We see that the water baptism was an outward expression of repentance and renewal and the Spirit baptism is an inward manifestation of forgiveness and transformation.

It is the Spirit, like water, that cleanses and washes away our sins, and like fire, in how it refines and purifies the soul.

Water baptism helps us to understand and appreciate the receiving of the Holy Spirit. The two work together and when they are understood together is amazing.

Some argue that water baptism is not necessary for salvation but only that you believe in Christ. I say if you believe in Christ, that faith is represented through water baptism.

Some believe you only need the Spirit baptism or Holy Spirit to be saved. I say, "how can you receive the Holy Spirit if you do not first proclaim your belief in God and Jesus."

I believe that both water baptism and spirit baptism have their place, significance, and meaning.

In the Bible, Christ explains to Nicodemus that to enter the Kingdom of God he must be born of water and spirit. *John 3:5 "Jesus answered, Verily, Verily, I say unto you, except a man be born of water and of the Spirit, he cannot enter into the kingdom of God."*

What did this mean? To be born of water and spirit? In this passage Christ is speaking about being reborn. We see a reference here to water and spirit like how we seen in *John 1:3 when John says he baptizes with water and Christ baptizes with the Holy Spirit and fire.*

Some argue that Christ is referring to water as physical birth and the spirit as spiritual rebirth. Others believe that Christ is referencing water and spirit both as rebirth and that we must be born again of water and of spirit, which is represented by baptism by water and baptism by spirit.

Nicodemus has a hard time understanding this thinking how someone can be reborn, asking should I go back into my mother's womb, which he was already thinking of the physical birth, however, Christ was speaking about being reborn of water and of spirit, giving reference to the baptism.

Was Christ saying that every man born must be reborn in the Spirit or was Christ giving reference to two baptisms that we must be reborn of water and of spirit?

Either, He is telling Nicodemus who is already born that he must be reborn of spirit to enter the Kingdom of God, or He is telling him you must be reborn of water and reborn of spirit?

Being reborn represents baptism, which is, being born again of water and born again of spirit. So, then he is telling Nicodemus if you are not baptized by water and baptized by Spirit, or born again of water and of spirit, then you cannot enter the Kingdom of God.

We see that the two are used together, water and spirit, and that we must proclaim our faith in Christ through baptism by water and receive the Holy Spirit through baptism by fire.

We can see this by John giving reference to water and spirit by fire, and how Christ also gives reference to water and spirit, which shows that together the water baptism and spirit baptism have their place, significance, and meaning.

The water baptism signifies our faith in Christ and the spirit baptism signifies the receiving of the Holy Spirit. Just as John was to prepare the way for Christ. The water baptism was to prepare us for the receiving of the Spirit.

Not only professing our faith in Christ and being reborn but preparing us as disciples to receive his Gift. Understanding how water is used helps us understand the spirit.

Christ usually spoke in parables giving an analogy of earthly things for heavenly things. The water here is symbolic of the spirit.

Understanding how water is poured out, cleanses and washes away dirt, and is represented as life, renewal, and rebirth helps us to understand how the Spirit is poured out, cleanses and washes away our sins, and is also represented as life, renewal, and rebirth.

The spirit baptism is represented by fire to differentiate between the water, in which, John knew that he baptized by water, so he describes Christ baptism of Holy Spirit with Fire. The Fire also helps us to understand the Spirit.

Understanding how we are consumed and engulfed in the Spirit that dwells within us and how it cleanses, refines, and purifies us, and is represented as life, renewal, rebirth, and transformation.

Some argue that you do not need to be baptized to be saved. Well let's look at some examples. First, Christ himself was baptized of water by John and commanded his disciples to go baptize nations in the name of Jesus in the great commission.

Jesus was the Way, the Truth, and the Light. He was showing us the way when he was baptized by water. Apostles baptized new believers and they received the Holy Spirit.

Christ spoke of being reborn of water and spirit. These examples show how water baptism is significant, in that, it proclaims first the belief in Christ. The spirit baptism by fire is significant, in that, it signifies the receiving of the Holy Spirit.

These two are used together to help us better understand the spirit, the death and resurrection of Christ, and the transformation.

It helps us to understand how the Spirit is poured out, washes away our sins, cleanses and refines us, purifies and sanctifies us, therefore, putting away the old self and being transformed in the new.

I love how both water and fire represent the Spirit and how they have their place, meaning, and significance.

Here is another reference to water and fire showing how we must pass through:

Isaiah 43:2 "When you pass through the waters, I will be with you; and through the rivers, they shall not overwhelm you; when you walk through the fire you shall not be burned, and the flame shall not consume you."

Numbers 31:23 "Everything that can stand the fire, you shall pass through the fire, and it shall be clean.

Nevertheless, it shall also be purified with the water for impurity. And whatever cannot stand the fire, you shall pass through the water."

Here we see water and fire being represented as something we will pass through, which is baptism, and that the water will not overwhelm you or the fire consume you. This water and fire are the baptism of Spirit. We see that the water and fire are both referenced in the cleansing and purifying process that we pass through.

In Conclusion, water and fire are both used to symbolize the Spirit. John's Baptism by water and Christ's baptism of Spirit by fire.

Christ told Nicodemus he must be reborn of water and spirit, in which, he was speaking of the baptisms John spoke about.

The water symbolizes our faith in Christ, the cleansing and washing away of sins, and renewal and rebirth. The fire represents the receiving of the Holy Spirit, the refining and purifying of sins, and rebirth and transformation.

Together they represent baptism and the passing through water and fire, which is, the two things that Christ told Nicodemus, that we must be born of water and of spirit.

Chapter 3
God's Law of Love

What is the Law of God? The Law of God is to love and above this there is no law. What is love? Love is patient, love is kind, love is forgiving, love comes from God, and God is love.

What are the Ten Commandments? The Ten Commandments or Law of Moses were commands given to God's people to warn against disobeying the law, in which, that disobedience is sin which leads to death.

The commandments outline what not to do, for instance, that you do not lie, cheat, and steal, whereby, these things are defined as evil, sin, and wickedness.

The law warns against these things by saying do not do them for they are sin and lead to death, however, by following the law and abiding in the law it leads to wisdom and righteousness.

The Law is Holy for it shows us what is right and outlines a moral code of conduct, however, the law of Moses is not perfect for it had not been fulfilled and was defined in sin.

What is the fulfilled law of Christ? The New Covenant represents the fulfilled law of Christ, in which, Christ removes sin from the law and gives us a new perfected law fulfilled in love.

Christ explains that God is love and that love fulfills the Law, therefore, the law of God is to love and that above this there is no law.

There is no law against love but there is a law against sin. The law stands as a guideline and basis to judge against sin by making clear what should be done and not be done.

In the new perfected law of Christ, He makes clear that love fulfills the law and shows us what we should do, which is, to first love God with all your heart, mind, and soul and second, to love your neighbor as yourself.

Christ says this fulfills the law of Moses for if you truly love God and your neighbor you would not harm, lie, cheat, or steal from your neighbor, but instead, you would love your neighbor the way God loves you and would be your brother's keeper, this love truly does fulfill the law.

The law taught us right from wrong, good from bad, and that going against the law leads to sin and punishment.

Christ came to teach us love and how to love, to walk in the spirit and not by the letter, and that through Christ who fulfills the law leads us to eternal life and salvation.

You may ask how can we love if we never know what love is? Or how can I have mercy and forgiveness without disobedience? The law came through disobedience, but Grace came through Jesus Christ.

Christ made known to us the Love of God by showing us that God forgives us and that He sent His only Son for us as salvation. God tells us to forgive others as He has forgiven us and to be merciful as God has shown mercy to us. God tells us to not judge or condemn others but love and correct each other as God loves and corrects us. This love shows us the ways of God and that God is love.

Gods Law is very similar to the rules of a house. For example, the father is the head of the household, he sets the rules in the house, he is the oldest and has the authority in the house for he is the creator of that household.

The father sets rules in the house and teaches and guides his children through principles and morals. He teaches them the right way to be and how to be safe in the world, how to be a man of good morals and to make wise decisions.

The father does this out of love for his children for he knows what is good for them. The rules are set to show what this house stands for and breaking or disobeying these rules have punishments.

As you became a teenager you may well have rebelled and became disobedient to your father's rules. If you disobey your father you may be punished, chastised, grounded, cast out, or even kicked out the house.

You can hear the voice of any father saying, "This is my house and my rules, you either abide by my rules or you can get out."

As we rebel and become disobedient to the rules of our father, we then get ourselves into trouble and through hard experiences we start to learn our lesson.

We may feel sorry for what we done and hope to come back home. If you truly feel sorry and apologize, your father would forgive you and allow you back home because he loves you unconditionally.

In the same manner, Gods laws serve as rules and principles of morality for humanity in His earth. God the Father is the head over all, He is the Creator of us all and has sovereign authority over all creation. He sets the rules and gives us the law to live by.

As a loving Father He shows us the right way to live and gives us the law to show us right from wrong. The law is the basis of morality and to follow it is wisdom. Our Father knows what is best for us and show us what is good.

The laws of God are like the rules of the house, with God being our Father, He gives us rules to live by to direct us and show us the right way to live and to warn us of the penalty of sin.

The Father sets the rules and shows us what and what not to do. He shows us what He stands for and what He expects of us. God is Good, Righteous, Fair, Just, Merciful and Loving.

His Law is to love and to pursue all righteousness, by doing no harm to each other nor taking from one another, by not lying to each another or slandering one another, but instead, by loving each other and giving to one another, and by being honest with each other and loyal to one another.

These are the rules of the house, the laws that God set before us as a guideline on how to treat each other in His house, for we are all brothers and sisters in God's house as His children.

If you follow the rules, then the Father will be pleased but if you break the rules then there will be punishment and you may be kicked out or cast out. A father would have to be firm and just and stand by his rule like any father would but would also have unconditional love for his children.

Although they break the rules God displays His love for His children by forgiving them and allowing them back into the home once they have learned their lesson, repented of their wrong doings, and asked for forgiveness.

This is the understanding of law and punishment and grace and mercy, the fall of man through sin and the reconciliation of man through grace.

That Gods law is the rules or guidelines given to us to follow to know what is right and wrong, moral and immoral, good and evil. The law was given as rules against sin and for disobedience.

Think of it this way, if a child is being good then you don't have to give him rules you just promote good behavior. On the other hand, if a child is being disobedient or unruly then you must set some rules and teach them what is right through law and order.

In the same manner, Gods law was given through the Israelites disobedience and stood as the law against sin and law of morality. We would not have the law if they had not disobeyed but we would not have grace if there was no disobedience.

Through disobedience we received the law and through grace we receive the spirit. For if disobedience came through the law then grace came through the perfect obedience and sacrifice of Jesus Christ.

The law was to be written on the hearts of men and through the renewing of the Holy Spirit. God dealt with His people to show us that through disobedience the law became sin and death but through the obedience of His Son the law was fulfilled.

Through His death He destroyed sin and death and became eternal life for us through the Spirit, therefore, setting us free from the condemnation of the law which is sin and death and bringing us into salvation through the law of Spirit and Life.

This helps to better understand being cast out and condemned for sin for breaking the rules or law and being forgiven and justified by our Father through His grace and mercy, therefore, receiving forgiveness and salvation and allowed back into the kingdom of God.

The law is set to show what God stands for and what He expects of us. If you break or disobey the law there are consequences and punishments, this disobedience is called sin.

The wages of sin is death which is the penalty that the law carries. This idea brings us to further understand that if we sin or disobey Gods law then there is punishment or condemnation. You could see it as being cast out or punished for your disobedience.

Obeying our Father pleases Him and brings us closer to Him, however, sin separates us from God and leaves us out in the dark. The understanding is that we have all sinned and disobeyed Gods law and we all are cast out from the house of God.

Our Father who loves us unconditionally has given us a Way to get back home, that if we repent and truly change our rebellious ways, He will forgive us and allow us into the Kingdom of God.

God is Our Father who loves us and teaches us through experiences in life, chastising and rewarding us in life, showing us that sin has immediate and long-term effects that lead to death.

He gives us the Law to protect us and keep us safe from evil, teaching us right from wrong, and that our actions have consequences.

These consequences which sometimes are immediate teach us the repercussions of bad behavior, that nothing good comes from sin, and that we learn from our mistakes and learn our lessons.

The long-term effect of sin is that it brings death. The wage of sin is death, but the gift of God is eternal life. The law through disobedience brought death, but by Grace through the death of Christ brings eternal life.

By the law we are reminded that we are not perfect and have been cut off or cast out due to sin and have been condemned to death.

It is by Grace we are saved through Christ Jesus and have been reconciled and brought back home due to God's mercy and salvation, that He loved us so much that He gave His only begotten Son that all who believe in Him shall have everlasting life.

Deuteronomy 10:12 "And now, Israel, what does the Lord your God require of you, but to fear the Lord your God, to walk in His ways, to serve the Lord your God with all your heart and with all your soul, to keep the commandments of the Lord and His statutes which I command you today for your good?

His Commandments are not a burden or weigh you down but are pleasant and carry a light load. His ways are Love, Truth, and Righteousness.

He did not command as if it is for His own good but rather for our own good. It is like a father who tell his children to "play nice", the law was given as counsel and a guideline for us to live by His Ways.

Christ said, "I did not come to destroy the law but to fulfill the law", for the Law is love, love God with all your heart, mind, and soul and love your neighbor.

For love fulfills the law, if you truly love your brother you would not steal from your brother, lie, cheat or kill your brother, you would not slander your brother's name, for it says "I am my brother's keeper" we keep the law for the love of God and we are delighted in His ways.

The ways of God are to love for God is love and is the source of love. What is love? Love is patient, love is kind, it does not envy, it does not boast, it is not proud, it is not rude, it is not self-seeking, it is not easily angered, keeps no record of wrongs, does not delight in evil, rejoices with the truth, always protects, always trusts, always hopes, always perseveres, and love never fails"

God is love and shows us His love, in which, He did not abandon nor forsake us but saved us and gave us eternal life and redemption through His Son.

1 John 4:7 'Beloved, let us love one another, for love is from God, and whoever loves has been born of God and knows God. Anyone who does not love does not know God, because God is love. In this the love of God was made manifest among us, that God sent his only begotten Son into the world, so that we might live through him."

In Conclusion, the law of God is to love for God is love and above this there is no law. The law or commandments stand as truth and righteousness, showing us right from wrong, and what we should do and not do.

The law also brought sin and death through disobedience, for the penalty of the law was death. In the New covenant law, Christ destroyed sin and death and fulfilled the law, giving us a new law that fulfills the old law, which is to love, for love fulfills the law.

In doing this we are freed from the bondage of the law which is sin and death and brought into the newness of Spirit which is eternal life through Jesus Christ.

Here are some scriptures for reference.

Romans 7:12 "So then, the law is Holy, and the commandments is holy, righteous and good."

1 John 5:2 "By this we know that we love the children of God: when we love God and keep His commandments. In fact, this is love for God: to keep his commands, and his commandments are not burdensome."

Matthew 5:17 Jesus explains "Think not that I am come to destroy the law, or the prophets: I am not come to destroy, but to fulfil. 18 For verily I say unto you, till heaven and earth pass, one jot or one tittle shall in no wise pass from the law, till all be fulfilled. 19 Whosoever therefore shall break one of these least commandments, and shall teach men so, he shall be called the least in the kingdom of heaven: but whosoever shall do and teach them, the same shall be called great in the kingdom of heaven."

Matthew 22:36 a man asked Jesus, "Teacher, which is the greatest commandment in the Law?" Jesus replied: "Love the Lord your God with all your heart and with all your soul and with all your mind. This is the first and greatest commandment. And the second is like it: 'Love your neighbor as yourself.' All the Law and the Prophets hang on these two commandments."

Romans 13:8-10 it explains how love is the fulfilling of the law, it says "Owe no one anything, except to love each other, for the one who loves another has fulfilled the law. For the commandments, "You shall not murder, you shall not steal, you shall not covet," and any other commandment, are summed up in this word: "You shall love your neighbor as yourself." Love does no wrong to a neighbor; therefore, love is the fulfilling of the law."

Chapter 4

Under Law or Under Grace

What does it mean to be under the law or to be under grace? To be under the Law means you are under the requirements and penalty of the law, which is the wages of sin is death. The law is good and is to be followed but if you break the law there is a penalty and judgement. The penalty of the law or punishment is death by law and that you are judged according to the law and your works. To be under grace means you are under the mercy and salvation of God. Grace is God forgiving us of our sins and justifying us according to His grace and righteousness. Grace pardons us from the penalty of the law which is death, and God's gift to us is eternal life through faith in Jesus Christ.

The law and grace are proportional to each other. As one increases the other decreases. The more you live under the law the less you have grace, or the more you live under grace the less you are under the law. In this case the law and grace are contrary to each other. The law represents self-righteous works and self-justification. God's grace represents His righteousness that saves us and is a justification that comes from God.

When I speak of law, I am not speaking of the commandments but of the penalty that the law carries. The law in this case is known as the law of sin and death, for through this law came sin and death, and for by the law the penalty or wages for sin is death. When I speak of grace, I am speaking of what God has done for us to free us from sin and the penalty of the law. Through God's grace we are redeemed and pardoned from the law.

Does this mean we do not follow Gods Law? Certainly not! For we know following His law leads to righteousness but by the law we cannot be saved for we are not perfect and in our flesh we have sinned. For all have fell short of the glory of God, but the gift of God is everlasting life. This means that although we fall short, God has forgiven us through His grace and mercy. Therefore, we are under God's grace and no longer under the law.

To be clear, we are under God's grace and by faith we are saved, by believing in His Son and following in His ways. We are set free and no longer under the law and its penalty but now live under Christ and have God's grace and salvation. I will investigate how the law and grace are proportional but equal respectively, just as works and faith are proportional but respectively equal. I will investigate what it means to be under the law or to be under grace.

Let us look and see what scripture has to say about law and grace so we can better understand what it means to be under the law and under grace.

Romans 6:14 For sin shall not be master over you, for you are not under the law but under grace.

Romans 7:4-5 Therefore, my brother, you also were made to die to the Law through the body of Christ, so that you might be joined to another, to Him who was raised from the dead, in order that we might bear fruit for God. For while were in the flesh, the sinful passions, which were aroused by the Law, were at work in the members of the body to bear fruit for death.

Romans 3:21 But now apart from the Law the righteousness of God has been manifested, being witnessed by the Law and the Prophets,

Romans 11:6 But if it is by grace, it is no longer on the basis of works, otherwise grace is no longer grace.

Galatians 5:4 You have been severed from Christ, you who are seeking to be justified by law; you have fallen from grace.

Galatians 3:18 For if the inheritance is based on law, it is no longer based on a Promise; but God has granted it to Abraham by means of a promise.

Galatians 5:18 But if you are led by the Spirit, you are not under the law.

Romans 4:5 But to the one who does not work, but believes in Him who justifies the ungodly, his faith is credited as righteousness,

Galatians 3:23-24 But before faith came, we were kept in custody under the law, being shut up to the faith which was later to be revealed. Therefore, the Law has become our tutor to lead us to Christ, so that we may be justified by faith.

John 1:17 For the Law was given through Moses; grace and truth were realized through Jesus Christ.

Romans 5:20 The Law came in so that the transgression would increase; but where sin increased, grace abounded all the more,

Galatians 2:21 "I do not nullify the grace of God, for if righteousness comes through the Law, then Christ died needlessly"

Romans 10:4 For Christ is the end of the law for righteousness to everyone that believeth.

Romans 7:7 What shall we say then? Is the law sin? God forbid. No, I had not known sin, but by the law;

Romans 3:31 Do we then make void the law through faith? God forbid: yea, we establish the law.

Romans 7:6 But now we are delivered from the law, that being dead wherein we were held; that we should serve in newness of spirit, and not in the oldness of the letter.

Galatians 3:10 For as many as are to the works of the law are under the curse: for it is written, cursed is every one that continue not in all things which are written in the book of the law to do them.

Romans 3:19 Now we know that what things the law says, it says to them who are under the law: that every mouth may be stopped, and all the world may become guilty before God.

James 2:10 For whosoever shall keep the whole law, and yet offend in one, he is guilty of all.

Romans 7:12 Wherefore the law is holy, and the commandment holy, and just, and good.

Romans 8:4 That the righteousness of the law might be fulfilled in us, who walk not after the flesh, but after the Spirit.

Galatians 5:18 But if you be led of the Spirit, you are not under the law.

Romans 8:1 There is therefore now no condemnation to them which are in Christ Jesus, who walk not after the flesh, but after the Spirit.

Galatians 2:16 Knowing that a man is not justified by the works of the law, but by the faith of Jesus Christ, even we have believed in Jesus Christ, that we might be justified by the faith of Christ, and not by the works of the law: for by the works of the law shall no flesh be justified.

Romans 3:28 Therefore we conclude that a man is justified by faith without the deeds of the law.

Ephesians 2:8 For by grace are you saved through faith; and that is not of yourselves: but it is the gift of God.

One source wrote, "Here, the terms "law" and "grace" are employed to designate the predominate systems of divine, written revelation--namely the two covenants.

The first covenant was that given through Moses at Sinai, commonly known as the law of Moses. The second was a universal covenant for mankind that issued from Jesus Christ and was ratified by the Lord's death. Jeremiah referred to these respective systems as "the covenant" that Jehovah made with the fathers when he brought them out of Egyptian bondage, and the "new covenant" which later would be world-wide in scope. The writer of Hebrews referred to these laws as the first and the second, or the old and the new. The two covenants are designated respectively as "law" and "grace." The function of the Mosaic law was as follows: 1. To demonstrate that the violation of divine law separates the perpetrator from God. 2. To declare that written law is needed to define sin. 3. To show, by recorded precedent, that sacred justice requires that a penalty be paid for law-breaking. On the other hand, the dominant design of the New Covenant is to stress the redemptive mission of Christ as the only remedy for the human sin problem. The wonderful plan of salvation is the result of Heaven's grace, not human merit. No richer term, than that of grace, could be employed as a synecdoche for the summation of God's thrilling plan of redemption. It is entirely reasonable, therefore, that these two systems should be set forth in a contrasted fashion, such as law and grace."

As we can see, law and grace are respectively proportional to each other, one is first and the other is second, one is old and the other is new, they are contrary to each other but equal in the same respects. There can't be the new without the old and the second without the first. The new replaces the old and the second replaces the first. As grace increases the law decreases, and where the law is increased, grace is decreasing.

This is in reference to being under the law or under grace. You are either under the law or under grace. Under the law means you have not accepted faith in Christ Jesus and God's grace, you believe your works under the law saves you. Under the law is a person who feels justified by their works or is self-righteous.

Under grace means you have accepted faith and salvation in Jesus Christ and are freed from the penalty of the law. Under grace means to live under Christ and the Law of Spirit and Life and to walk in the Spirit. Under grace means to believe that it is God who saves you and justifies you through faith, not by works of the law, but in this faith, you produce good fruit. This is being justified by faith and is the righteousness of God.

So, yes! then you say "I am under grace and by faith I follow God's ways and keep His Law written on my heart. I am no longer under the law and its penalty but have been set free through Jesus Christ and live a new life in Christ free of sin, not free to sin but free from sin." I will investigate a few examples of how law and grace work together.

I would like to look at the story where Jesus was talking to the prostitute. This event shows a good correlation between law and grace. For example, the woman who was guilty of adultery was being condemned by the people, according to the law, they were to stone her to death as a penalty for breaking the law. Jesus knew what they were thinking and asked them whoever here is without sin cast the first stone. Jesus knew that every person there has sinned, so he knew no one could cast a stone. This explains how no man is perfect and by law we are condemned to death according to the penalty of the law. The only person there that was without sin, was Jesus Christ, and He was the only person that could rightfully judge her. As we can see Christ did not condemn her nor judge her for her sins, instead he extended grace and forgiveness to her. She was on her knees pleading to the Lord to forgive her, she had confessed of her sin to Jesus, and in turn Christ says, "you have been forgiven, now get up and go serve the Lord."

As we can see Christ did not judge her nor condemn her according to the law but gave her forgiveness and salvation according to grace. This explains the relationship between law and grace, that the law condemns and ends in judgment, but grace from God through Christ Jesus forgives and gives us salvation.

We know that we are judged according to the law for every man will be judged according to his works, good or bad. However, it is not that we be condemned under the law but be justified by God through grace, faith, and salvation in Jesus Christ. This explains how by the law no man will be justified, but by faith in Jesus Christ we are justified by Grace.

"He that is without sin" is a reminder that we are not perfect under the law and to remind us that Christ was without sin. The law condemns and the Pharisees would have stoned her to death under the penalty of the law, but the only one that could technically throw a stone was Christ for He is without sin. Under grace He did not condemn her to death by stoning, but instead forgave her and showed her mercy and grace then said "Now go and serve the Lord" this was an example of how law and grace works.

Through Moses came the law and judgement and through Christ came grace and salvation. Under the law she would have been stoned but under grace she was saved. Under the law she was condemned and had no hope but under grace she was forgiven and gained hope through faith. Christ forgave her and told her to serve him. He does not say "I forgive you, now go and keep on sinning", but He does say "I forgive you, now go and serve the Lord."

When we think of law we think of order, we imagine a courtroom with lawyers; the prosecutor who accuses and the defense attorney who defends, and we envision a judge and a jury who uses the law to issue punishments. Just imagine how law and grace act very much like a court of law.

For example, in a court of law, if you commit a crime and are found guilty under the law, you are sentenced to a judgement according to the law. Although you are guilty you will ask for the court's mercy and hope the judge is lenient that you may be in the graces of the court.

In some cases, the judge will approve a pardon, or someone will take the charge for you and pay the penalty for that crime. In that case, you are technically no longer guilty because someone has taken your punishment for you and you are pardoned. In that event, you would feel indebted to that person who saved you. You would not or should not commit that crime again but be thankful that you were forgiven and pardoned.

In the same manner, we have a Righteous and Fair Judge in the Courts of Heaven in the presence of Angels, whereby, we are all charged and guilty of sin, and under the law we are condemned to death. The penalty of sin is death, but through God's grace comes everlasting life.

We have been pardoned by God through His Son, and in doing so we willingly serve God and rejoice! Knowing that we have been forgiven and freed from the penalty of the law and guilt of sin and allows us to walk in Spirit and newness of life, having His Law written on our hearts. Also, knowing that God is not cruel but loving and lenient, like a good Father and fair judge.

The law condemns while grace saves. One precedes the other. The Law shows God's justice and righteousness, while Grace shows God's mercy and love. We should keep the law written on our hearts and be under God's grace. Christ said He did not come to abolish the law but to fulfill it. That through Christ the law is fulfilled, and under Christ we follow the law of Christ, which the first commandment is to love God with all your heart, mind, and soul, so that is to keep His laws written on our hearts and follow in His ways.

The difference between law and grace is the mentality and the legality, for instance, the law says you are guilty of sin and await judgement while grace says you are pardoned of sin now go and serve God. One condemns and judges while the other forgives and shows mercy.

Think of it this way, God doesn't want to force us by law to serve him out of fear but gives us free will to choose to serve him out of love. How would you feel forcing someone to love you or giving them the choice? To have God's Grace is to willingly keep his law and not be under condemnation but instead, under His Grace and Salvation.

The law of Moses was God's standard on holiness and righteousness, although the law was to be broken knowing that none of us are perfect. The law is good and stands as a guideline to moral judgement. The Law displays God's justice and judgement and shows His righteousness. The law reminds us that we are not perfect and are in need of a savior. To fulfill the law, one would have to be without sin. This is how Christ was able to fulfill the law, that through Christ we escape the condemnation of the law and come into God's grace through Jesus Christ.

I want to clear up that I am not saying to sin under grace or that grace replaces the law. Christ said I come not to abolish or destroy the law but to fulfill it. He says the Law, which is the Law of Christ, can be summed up in two. Love

God with all your heart, mind, and soul and to love your neighbor as yourself. In doing this you will fulfill the law for love fulfills the law.

We are no longer under the Law of sin and death and the law of condemnation and judgement. However, we are under God's grace under the Law of Spirit and Life and the law of forgiveness and mercy. The law is good and to be followed, there is wisdom in the law, and it leads to righteousness.

The law brought a mentality or bondage to the law, whereby, the law is defined in sin. The new law of Christ just redefines the old law but removes the penalty and removes sin from the law. To love God and your neighbor is truly fulfilling the law. The Grace of God is the Mercy of God and understanding that God has justified and redeemed us through faith according to His Righteousness. It is this mentality that frees us from bondage of the law and sets us free in His grace. It is understanding that we have been forgiven and have received God's grace through His Son, that we have been redeemed and justified by God.

Understanding that we get up and serve the Lord, follow His Law of Love, and keep His commands written on our hearts. Therefore, living under the Grace of God is keeping in His ways, walking in the Spirit of grace, and producing good fruit through faith and good works. This is the relationship between law and grace and how they are respectively proportional to each other.

Chapter 5

Faith that Produces Good Fruit

I walk into a room and there are three people who have three different perspectives on the relationship between faith and works. I ask the first person what do they believe about faith and works? The first person says, "I don't believe in God, but I believe I am a good person."

I ask the other two people the same question. The second person says, "I believe in God and that faith alone saves, I don't need good works only faith to be saved."

The last person says, "I believe in God and believe that one's faith is proven by their good works but that it is faith alone that saves you not good works."

After hearing all their responses, I began to see the different perspectives people have about faith and works. In this chapter I will be looking into the topic of faith and works and to see how true faith produces good fruit.

What is faith? It is the belief in the One True God and faith in His Son, Christ Jesus. What are good works? Good works are the good deeds of a person, it is the self-righteous acts of a man.

What is faith without works? It is having a faith that doesn't produce good works, it is a dead faith, for faith without works is dead. It is claiming you have faith, but it is not proven by actions. What is works without faith? It is having good works without faith. Doing good deeds and being a good person but lacking or having no faith in God or in His Son. It is claiming you are a good person or self-righteous and don't need to believe in God or in the salvation and justification given by God. Works without Faith is dead, for a person's good deeds mean nothing if you have no faith in God.

What is faith alone saves? This is the understanding that faith in the perfect sacrifice of Jesus Christ was deemed worthy by God and that God justifies us by faith alone. God is Just and the Justifier and it is by us having faith in what God did for us, not what we did for God, that saves us.

What is true faith? True faith is a faith that produces good deeds or better known as good fruit. It is believing in God and in the redemption that comes through Christ Jesus, it is a faith that produces good fruit.

For example, good works are good deeds done without faith; good fruits are good deeds done in faith. Good works are self-righteous works and good fruit are good works which come from faith and the Fruits of the Spirit. Good fruit are the good works that we produce in good faith, it is a true faith that produces good fruit. It is a good work that is being produced in us once we have faith.

What does faith without works is dead mean? If you cannot prove your faith with actions, then your faith means nothing. If a person believes or has faith in something it must be proven by their actions.

For example, if I believe and claim that I don't like mustard then I cannot eat mustard because it goes against what I believe in. If my actions go against my faith, then on the contrary it becomes hypocritical. You cannot have faith without works for your good deeds prove your faith.

Some say all I need is faith and that I don't need good works, that faith alone saves, and that I don't have to be a good person because my faith saves me. To have faith without works is dead, it is by having a true faith that produces good fruit that saves.

In the book of James he says, "faith without works is like the body without the Spirit." What this means is that as a body without a spirit is dead, as well, your faith without works is dead.

What does works without faith is dead mean? If you are a good person who does good deeds but has no faith in God or salvation, then your self-righteous deeds mean nothing. If a person believes that their good works save them and not have faith in God's salvation, then their works are fruitless and lack faith, and works without faith is dead.

For example, I am a good person, but I believe my good deeds make me worthy of salvation not understanding that it is faith in Gods perfect sacrifice that has made me worthy. It is not by my own good works that I am saved, but by God who saves me through His Son, where God is the Justifier and Redeemer. It is not a self-justification but a justification that comes from God by faith.

Titus 3:5 "He saved us, not because of works done by us in righteousness, but according to his own mercy, by the washing of regeneration and renewal of the Holy Spirit."

Galatians 2:16 'Yet we know that a person is not justified by works of the law but through faith in Jesus Christ, so we also have believed in Christ Jesus, in order to be justified by faith in Christ and not by works of the law, because by works of the law no one will be justified."

Romans 3:25 "God presented Christ as a sacrifice of atonement, through the shedding of his blood- to be received by faith. He did this to demonstrate his righteousness, because in his forbearance he had left the sins committed beforehand unpunished--he did it to demonstrate his righteousness at the present time, so as to be just and the justifier of those who have faith in Jesus."

You cannot claim to be good or have good works and not have faith in the very source of all goodness. To lack faith makes your works void and that they mean nothing if you don't first have faith in God. Works without faith is dead and produces no fruit, these works are faithless and fruitless.

In James it says "What good does it do, if someone claims to have faith but does not prove it with actions? This kind *of faith cannot save him, can it? Faith, by itself, if it does not prove itself with actions, is dead."*

What is a faith that produces good fruit? This is a true faith that produces the Fruits of the Spirit. These are good deeds done in good faith. These are the good deeds we produce in Christ and are offered as fruit to God, it is the manifestation of the Holy Spirit within us.

The Fruits of the Spirit are described as kindness, gentleness, humbleness, meekness, patience, self-control and these are the good deeds that come from the Spirit. These fruits represent our faith and identify us as having a faith that produces good fruit. This true faith is identified by its fruit just as a tree is identified by its fruit.

A good tree produces good fruit just as a good faith will produce good fruit. This true faith understands that faith alone saves but a faith that produces good fruit in Christ. That it is not our good works that save us but by having faith in Christ and in the salvation of God that saves us, and that this faith will cause us to follow in the ways of God.

Although we are not perfect and fall short of the glory of God, we know that we are forgiven and justified by God allowing us to willingly live for God and do our best to follow in His ways, knowing that God strengthens us through His Spirit and also justifies us by His Grace.

Faith that produces good fruit is having faith first and good works or fruit that follow, it is a true faith that is faithful and fruitful.

John 15:5 "I am the vine; you are the branches. If you remain in me and I in you, you will bear much fruit; apart from me you can do nothing. 6 If you do not remain in me, you are like a branch that is thrown away and withers; such branches are picked up, thrown into the fire and burned. 7 If you remain in me and my words remain in you, ask whatever you wish, and it will be done for you. 8 This is to my Father's glory, that you bear much fruit, showing yourselves to be my disciples.

In the book of James, he addresses the issue between faith and works. He begins by saying that works without faith is dead and that faith without works is dead. He then explains how it is by faith alone that we are saved but also says a faith that is not proven by works is useless. So, it is understood that only a true faith that is proven by works or deeds is the faith alone that saves.

James 2:14 "What good is it, my brothers, if someone says he has faith but does not have works? Can that faith save him?

James 2:17 "So also faith by itself, if it does not have works, is dead.

James 2:18 "But someone will say, "You have faith and I have works." Show me your faith apart from your works, and I will show you my faith by my works."

James 2:20 "You foolish person, do you want evidence that faith apart from works is useless?"

James 2:21-23 "Was not Abraham our father justified by works, when he had offered Isaac upon the altar? Do you see that faith was working together with his works, and by works faith was made perfect? And the scripture was fulfilled that says, "Abraham believed God, and it was accounted to him as righteousness," and he was called God's friend.

James 2:24 "You see that a person is considered righteous by what they do and not by faith alone."

We can see that Abraham was counted as righteous for his faith but that his faith was working together with his works. When Abraham believed God, he had faith and when he showed God that he would sacrifice Isaac that was his work that proved his faith and by that faith he was accounted as righteous.

So, we see how his works had proved his faith but it was by his faith that he was considered righteous because he believed and trusted God. We see his faith came first and then was proven by his actions or his work.

We see that works apart from faith is dead and that faith apart from works is useless. So, we see that faith and works go together and work together in tandem. You can't have works then faith you should have faith then works. With faith coming first then fruit or good works that follow.

Source from gotquestions.com states, "Some see a difference between Paul (salvation is by faith alone) and James (salvation is by faith plus works). Paul dogmatically says that justification is by faith alone, while James appears to be saying that justification is by faith plus works. This apparent problem is answered by examining what exactly James is talking about. James is refuting the belief that a person can have faith without producing any good works. James is emphasizing the point that genuine faith in Christ will produce a changed life and good works. James is not saying that justification is by faith plus works, but rather that a person who is truly justified by faith will have good works in his/her life. If a person claims to be a believer, but has no good works in his/her life, the he/she likely does not have genuine faith in Christ.

Paul says the same thing in his writings. The good fruit believers should have in their lives is listed in Galatians 5:22-23. Immediately after telling us that we are saved by faith, not works, Paul informs us that we were created to do good works. Paul expects just as much of a changed life as James does: "Therefore, if anyone is in Christ, he is a new creation; the old has gone, the new has come." James and Paul do not disagree in their teaching regarding salvation. They approach the same subject from different perspectives. Paul simply emphasized that justification is by faith alone while James put emphasis on the fact that genuine faith in Christ produces good works."

We see that justification is by faith alone for salvation but faith that is not proven by good works is not genuine. So, it is a true faith that produces good fruit in Christ.

You can't have faith in your own works but should have faith in Christ alone for salvation which produces good works within us. Proving that we are His and proving our faith.

Faith alone saves means we are justified by faith in Christ alone for salvation. Faith plus works is showing how that faith is proven or considered genuine.

Chapter 6

Shadow of Things to Come

What is a shadow? What does a shadow represent? A shadow gives you a hint as to what is coming and gives you an idea of what is unseen or a soon to be reality.

In *Colossians 2:17 it states, "These are a shadow of the things that were to come; the reality, however, is found in Christ."*

What is the shadow of things to come? What does this mean? Well think of a shadow that is cast out in front of you, it is not you but only a shadow of you. Normally if someone is walking towards you, you would see their shadow first, then shortly after you would see the reality of the actual person who was casting the shadow. This passage of scripture is used to describe how things of old were a shadow of the things to come and how they are fulfilled in Christ.

In *Colossians 2:16 Paul says,* "Therefore do not let anyone judge you by what you eat or drink, or with regard to a religious festival, a New Moon celebration or a Sabbath day." He continues to say that *"These are a shadow of the things to come and the reality of these things are found in Christ."*

The shadows are previous events and traditions that lead to the reality of future events and the fulfilment of these traditions. Prophecy is a good example, as it foretells future events and that later prophecy is fulfilled. In the Old Testament there are many prophecies that are fulfilled in the New Testament.

The Passover, the Sabbath, the Law of Moses, and the Old Covenant were all shadows of what was to come and to be fulfilled in Christ, through The Last Supper, The Lords Day of Rest, the Law of Christ, and the New Covenant.

I will look further into each of these and how they are shadows of what was to come, and the reality and the fulfillment of these things is found in Christ.

The Passover of the Old testament is an event that is remembered to this day as when God delivered His people from bondage in Egypt. The Passover is when God told the Hebrews to put the blood of a lamb over their doorway and that the Angel of Death would pass over them, in which, they would be saved from death through the blood of the lamb. It is by this blood that they are saved and how their sins are covered and forgiven. This event is celebrated by Jews as the Passover and each year they have a religious festival where the High Priest would sacrifice the blood of a lamb for the forgiveness of sins.

Hebrews 10:1 For since the law has but a shadow of the good things to come instead of the true form of these realities, it can never, by the same sacrifices that continually offered every year, make perfect those who draw near."

The Passover was a shadow of what was to come, which was the Lamb of God that would be the High Priest, who sacrifices once and for all His blood for the forgiveness of sins that would not just cover sins but wash away sins.

Hebrews 9:12 He did not enter by means of the blood of goats and calves; but he entered the Most Holy Place once and for all by his blood, thus obtaining eternal redemption for us."

The Passover is fulfilled through Christ at the Last Supper, where Christ becomes the Passover Lamb, where He is seen as the Lamb of God who takes away the sins of the world. The Last Supper was on the day of Passover and signifies the transition from the symbolic ritual of Passover to the reality of Christ in the Last Supper. The reality is that Christ is the fulfillment of the Passover, in that, He is the Passover Lamb and it is His perfect blood that saves us from death and forgives us of our sins. God required animal sacrifices to provide a temporary covering of sins and to foreshadow the perfect and complete sacrifice of Jesus Christ. Christ says at the Last Supper; this is my body and my blood which has been given up for you.

1 Corinthians 11:24 "and when he had given thanks, he broke it and said, "This is my body, which is given up for you; do this in remembrance of me." 25 In the same way, after supper he took the cup saying, "This cup is the new covenant in my blood; do this, whenever you drink it, in remembrance of me."

In the Passover it is through blood that their sins are covered and forgiven and are saved from death and free from bondage. In the same manner, it is through the Lamb of God, Jesus Christ, who was sacrificed for us and by His blood we are saved from death and our sins are forgiven and washed away, in which, we are set free from the bondage of sin and death.

The Passover was just a shadow of what was to come in the reality fulfilled in Christ at the Last Supper. This was foreshadowing the once and for all sacrifice which Jesus Christ offered on the cross. Once this sacrifice was made there was no longer a need for the blood of animals. The blood of Christ is the basis of the New Covenant and shows the transition from the Passover to the Last Supper.

The Sabbath is the seventh day that God rested from all His works of Creation. *Genesis 2:2 And on the seventh day God ended His work which He had done, and He rested on the seventh day from all His work which He had done." 3 Then God blessed the seventh day and sanctified it,".* It is the day He told Moses in the Law, the fourth commandment, to be a day of rest and to be remembered throughout all time that on the seventh day God rested from all His works. *Exodus 20:8 "Remember the Sabbath day by keeping it Holy. 9 Six days you shall labor and do all your work 10 but the seventh day is a Sabbath to the Lord your God. On it you shall not do any work."*

The Sabbath was later related to the Hebrews and the exile from Egypt. They were exiled during the night of the Sabbath and this day was remembered as when God freed His people from bondage.

Exodus 20:1 And God spoke all these words: 2 "I am the Lord your God, who brought you out of Egypt, out of the land of slavery."

The Jews celebrate the Sabbath every Saturday, which is the last day of the week or seventh day. This day they rest and remember all what God created and how He freed them from bondage. This day represented their rest after years of bondage.

The Sabbath is celebrated from Friday evening to Saturday evening which represents how they escaped bondage during the night. The Sabbath is later transitioned into the Lord's Sabbath or the Lord's Day of Rest. This is the reality and fulfillment of the Sabbath through Christ.

On the day of Passover, that Friday evening Christ our Lord and Savior died for our sins, giving up his body and blood for us, and it was finished. Death is defeated and through Christ and through his blood we are saved from the bondage of sin and death. The next day, the Sabbath day Christ laid rest in the tomb of Joseph, just as prophecy predicted.

This is the day that Jesus rested from all His works on the earth, just as God rested from all His works. This day is the Lord's Day of Rest or the Lord's Sabbath. The Sabbath was now fulfilled in Christ.

The Sabbath was just a shadow of what was to come, which is, the Lord's Day of Rest. The Sabbath will always be remembered as the day God rested from all His works, the day God's people rested from bondage, and the day

Christ rested from all His works and sets us free from bondage through his blood. The Lord's Day of Rest is the fulfillment of the Sabbath.

The Mosaic Law, or the Law, that was given to Moses by God, the Ten Commandments, which also represents the Old Covenant or the Law. The Law was God's moral standpoint and guideline to judge against sin and as a basis of morality. The Law of Moses is also known as the Law of Sin and Death, whereby, under the law was the penalty of death by sin. For the wages of sin is death.

Romans 6:23 For the wages of sin is death, but the free gift of God is eternal life in Christ Jesus our Lord."

So, if under the law you sin you therefore break the covenant and are condemned to death. The law is good in that it shows us what is wrong, however, it also defines sin. For example, do not steal, do not lie, do not kill, are the Law and it stands as good but also defines what is evil. For sin can never be forgotten if we are reminded of what it is. For this reason, the law could not be kept perfectly, for no man is perfect. So, we all are condemned to death through sin according to the law.

Romans 7:12 but, because we cannot keep God's law on our own, the result is only sin and death for those under the law."

For this reason, the law was just a shadow of what was to come, which is, a better law and new covenant that would be fulfilled through Christ.

Hebrews 8:7 For if there had been nothing wrong with that first covenant, no place would have been sought for another."

Hebrews 9:15 For this reason Christ is the mediator of a new covenant, that those who are called may receive the promised eternal inheritance. For Christ died to set us free from the penalty of the sins they had committed under that first covenant."

Hebrews 10:9 Then He said, "Here I am, I have come to do your will." He takes away the first, that he may establish the second."

This is describing how the old practices of the Old Covenant were now fulfilled in Christ and that through His blood He establishes the New Covenant. Christ said, *"I did not come to abolish the law or do away with the law, I have come to fulfil the law."*

Although He establishes a new covenant through His blood and frees us from sin and death, He does not do away with God's Law but transitions the Law of Moses to the Law of Christ. The Law of Moses was a shadow of what was to come, in which, the Law of Christ overshadows and fulfills the Law of Moses.

The Law of Christ is to love God with all your heart, mind, and soul, and to love your neighbor. Love fulfills the Law, in that, if you love your neighbor you would not steal from your neighbor or lie to your neighbor. The Law of Christ is not defining sin but instead has transitioned it into a definition of love, so that all we see in the Law is to love.

No longer defining sin with "Do not lie" but now He says, "Be honest" showing us how to love.

John 4:7 "Beloved, let us love one another, for love is from God, and whoever loves has been born of God and knows God. Anyone who does not love does not know God, because God is Love."

John 5:3 "This is love for God: to obey His commands. And His commands are not burdensome."

The law of the Spirit or law of Love is not burdensome, in which, His commands are to Love, not doing away with the Law but rather having it written on our hearts and fulfilled in us. What we do away with is the sin, death, and condemnation that came from the old law and replacing it with the new renewed law by Christ through grace and salvation.

Romans 7:6 "But now, by dying to what once bound us, we have been released from the law so that we serve in the new way of the Spirit, and not in the old way of the written code."

The Law of Moses was fulfilled through Christ as the Law of Christ or Law of the Spirit. The Ten Commandments are still in effect and have not been done away with but are fulfilled through Christ in love. We are no longer under the Law of Sin and Death but through the New Covenant are under the Law of Spirit and Life through grace and salvation.

Romans 8:2 "because through Christ Jesus the law of the Spirit who gives life has set you free from the law of sin and death."

The Law of Moses was a shadow of what was to come, therefore, foreshadowed the reality that Christ would fulfill the Law of Moses and the Old Covenant, in which, the Law of Christ, the Law of the Spirit, and the New Covenant are fulfilled in Christ.

There are other references of Christ being the fulfillment of foreshadowing events. One reference is that Christ is the Rock and another that He is the Bread of Life. The Rock is first referenced in Exodus where Moses struck and sprang forth water for the Israelites while they were in the wilderness.

In Exodus 17:6 "Behold, I will stand before you there on the rock at Horeb, and you shall strike the rock, and water shall come out of it, and the people will drink." And Moses did so, in the sight of the elders of Israel."

This rock which is the source from where the flowing water sprang from, was life to the Israelites who were dying of thirst.

Exodus 17:3 "there was no water for the people to drink. Therefore, the people quarreled with Moses and said, "Give us water to drink." And Moses said to them, "Why do you quarrel with me? Why do you test the Lord?" But the people thirsted there for water, and the people grumbled against Moses and said, "Why did you bring us up out of

Egypt, to kill us and our children and our livestock with thirst?"

We can see that this water was a source of life for the people. This event was to help us understand how Christ fulfills these things. Christ is the Rock and from Him flows water of everlasting life. That any who drink of this water will never thirst again. He is the source from which everlasting life flows through, which is, a Rock given to us by God.

John 4:13-14 "Jesus said to her, "Everyone who drinks of this water will be thirsty again, but whoever drinks of the water that I will give him will never be thirsty again. The water that I will give him will become in him a spring of water welling up to eternal life."

1 Corinthians 10:4 "For they drank from the Spiritual Rock that followed them, and the Rock was Christ."

Just like the rock at Horeb that gave water as a source of life for the Israelites, it was also a foreshadowing event of Christ being the Rock, whereby, through Him comes flowing water of everlasting life.

Psalms 114:8 "He who turned the rock into a pool of water; yes, a spring of water flowed from solid rock."

Christ is also referred to as the Bread of Life. In the Bible, there was manna that came down from heaven and was the bread of life that the Israelites were given by God in the wilderness. This event is also foreshadowing and leading to Christ being the Bread of Life, that came down from heaven and was given to us by God.

In Exodus 16, the Lord said to Moses, "Behold, I am about to rain bread from heaven for you, and the people shall go out and gather a day's portion every day, that I will test them, whether they walk in my ways or not."

This bread is from heaven and came down as a source of food for the people, known as the Manna from Heaven or Bread of Life.

Psalms 78:23-25 "Yet He commanded the skies above and opened the doors of heaven, and he rained down on them manna to eat and gave them the grain of heaven. Man ate of the bread of the angels; he sent them food in abundance."

The bread was an abundant source of food for the Israelites who were dying of hunger.

Exodus 16 "And the whole congregation of the people of Israel grumbled against Moses and Aaron in the wilderness, and the people of Israel said to them, "Would that we had died by the hand of the Lord in the land of Egypt, when we sat by the meat pots and ate bread to the full, for you have brought us out into this wilderness to kill this whole assembly with hunger."

This bread was a source of life for the people. We can see some connections here in how they were dying of thirst and hunger in the wilderness, and they were given the Rock and Manna from Heaven as a source of life. Likewise, this event also helps us to understand how Christ is the

Bread of Life that came down from heaven given to us by God. This bread, just like the rock, is the source from which comes everlasting life.

John 6:31 "Our ancestors ate the manna in the wilderness; as it is written: 'He gave them bread from heaven to eat." Jesus said to them, 'Very truly I tell you, it is not Moses who has given you the bread from heaven, but it is my Father who gives you the true bread from heaven. For the bread of God is the bread that comes down from heaven and gives life to the world." Then Jesus declared, "I am the bread of life. Whoever comes to me will never go hungry, and whoever believes in me will never be thirsty."

The bread is not just physical bread for the physical body but a spiritual bread from heaven for the spiritual body. That man does not live off bread alone, but off the very Living Word of God. Christ is the Living Word of God and through Him we have life everlasting.

Deuteronomy 8:3 "And he humbled you and let you hunger and fed you with manna, which you did not know, nor did your fathers know, that he might make you know that man does not live by bread alone, but man lives by every word that comes from the mouth of the Lord."

This means that bread alone is for physical life but to have everlasting life is through the Word of God. We see that the manna from heaven and the bread of life, are represented as Christ, being the Bread of Life, the very Living Word of God, that came down from heaven and in Him is everlasting life. We see that no man who eats of this bread will hunger and no man who drinks of this water will thirst. As we can see this bread and water represent life, however, through Christ it represents the fulfillment of the manna from heaven and the rock that springs up eternal life. The rock at Horeb and the manna from Heaven were a prophetic foreshadowing of the reality that Christ is the Rock and the Bread of Life.

Another foreshadowing event was the account of Abraham having to sacrifice his one and only son Isaac for God. As we know Christ is the Lamb of God and the Son of God that takes away the sins of the world. This event is prophetic and foreshadows the coming of the Promise to Abraham and the Lamb that God will provide. In Genesis, Abraham is told by God, as a test, to sacrifice his only son Isaac as an offering.

Genesis 22:1 "Sometime later God tested Abraham. He said to him, "Abraham!" "Here I am," he replied. 2 Then God said, "Take your son, your only son, whom you love - Isaac- and go to the region of Moriah. Sacrifice him there as a burnt offering on a mountain I will show you"

As Abraham and Isaac were walking to the mountain Isaac ask his father where is the lamb that we must sacrifice, unaware that he is the sacrifice, Abraham tells Isaac that God will provide the Lamb.

Genesis 22:6 "Abraham took the wood for the burnt offering and placed it on his son Isaac, and he himself carried the fire and the knife. As the two of them went on together, 7 Isaac spoke up and said to his father Abraham,

"Father?" "Yes, my son?" Abraham replied. "The fire and wood are here," Isaac said, "but where is the lamb for the burnt offering?" 8 Abraham answered, "God himself will provide the lamb for the burnt offering, my son." and the two went on together."

God then tells Abraham to stop and not sacrifice his son but that it was a test to see if Abraham was faithful to God. When God seen the faith of Abraham, He made a Promise to bless Abraham and all his offspring.

Genesis 22:10 "Then he reached out his hand and took the knife to slay his son. 11 but the angel of the Lord called out to him from heaven, "Abraham, Abraham!" "Here I am," he replied. 12 Do not lay a hand on the boy," he said. "Do not do anything to him. Now I know that you fear God, because you have not withheld from me your son, your only son." 13 Abraham went over and took a ram and sacrificed it as a burnt offering instead of his son. 14 So Abraham called that place The Lord Will Provide. 15 The angel of the Lord called to Abraham from heaven a second time 16 and said, "I swear by myself, declares the Lord, that because you have done this and have not withheld your son, your only son, 17 I will surely bless you and make your descendants as numerous as the stars in the sky and as the sand on the seashore. 18 and through your offspring all nations will be blessed, because you have obeyed me."

As we can see Abraham was to sacrifice his one and only son for God, likewise, God would sacrifice His one and only Son for us all. Abraham said God will provide the lamb, and that Lamb, is the one and only Son of God, Jesus

Christ. When God seen that Abraham would sacrifice his only son for Him, God in return promises to bless Abraham and all nations by giving us His one and only Son, whereby, through Him we have everlasting life.

This is the Promise and the Blessing that is given to Abraham. The Promise that God would send his Son as a sacrifice and that through Him all nations will be blessed. That Promise is Christ and the Blessing is everlasting life, in which, through Jesus Christ we have the Promise of Eternal Life. This event indeed shows the faith of Abraham but also foreshadows the coming of Christ. The reality of Christ in this event, is that, He is the Promise, the One and Only Son of God, and The Lamb of God, that God provided for us.

In Conclusion, we see that the shadow of things to come were just foreshadowing events that lead to the reality and fulfilment of these things in Christ. We see how Christ is the Passover Lamb of the Old Covenant, that Christ our Lord rested on the Sabbath day, and that the Law of Christ fulfills the Law of Moses by His blood, which fulfills the New Covenant. The events of the Old Testament were foreshadowing the coming events of Christ in the New Testament.

The many prophecies of the Old Testament were pointing to Christ in the New Testament. From the rock at Horeb, the Manna from heaven, the Lamb that God will provide, which lead to the reality and fulfillment of Christ, in which, He is The Rock, The Bread of Life, and the Lamb of God.

The many events, or traditions and rituals, in the old testament were only a shadow of what was to come in Christ.

Just as prophecy is fulfilled and can be looked back on shows the grandness of how God works. In the same way, we can look back on the Sabbath, the Passover, and the Old Covenant and better understand and appreciate what was to come. These shadows help us to understand how Christ fulfills these things and how we can learn from the past.

These foreshadowing or prophetic events all lead to the reality of Christ. We understand that we should not live in the shadows but come out from the shadows into the glorious light of Christ. To understand that what is old is slowly being done away with and being waxed over with the new.

That the Law of Moses was perfected through the Law of Christ. That we should not mix new wine with old vessels, in case the new wine become spoiled. That what is made new is better than the former, *'For if that first covenant had been faultless, then should no place be sought for the second."* The new covenant perfected the law and the old covenant.

These shadows of events lead us to the reality of Christ. Therefore, Paul says, *"Do not let anyone judge you according to what you eat or drink, or a religious festival, a New Moon or Sabbath Day. For these things were just a shadow of the things to come in the reality and fulfillment of Christ."*

Chapter 7

Unity through Separation

In the Garden of Eden there was the Tree of Knowledge of Good and Evil. What is the Tree of Knowledge of Good and Evil? This tree represents Adam and Eve receiving knowledge of what is good and evil through disobedience. The Garden of Eden was known as Paradise and Adam and Eve lived eternally and only knew what was good until they ate from the tree and received knowledge of not only what was good but also what was evil.

Why was this done? If you know the Genesis story then you know that Eve was deceived by the Serpent and disobeyed the only commandment, which was to not eat from the Tree of Knowledge of Good and Evil. You can see that Paradise was interrupted by Satan as he deceived Adam and Eve to disobey God and bring evil into the world.

Well, how did God plan to fix this? Now that they know Good and Evil and Gods creation has been tainted, would He abandon them and start over or save them and justify them?

God's plan was for salvation through His Son, that through Christ we receive the Knowledge of God, which is, that God did not abandon nor forsake us but offered us Mercy and Grace through His Son, that Good prevails over Evil, and that we are His through redemption, faith, and his complete work.

I referenced the Garden of Eden story because I will base this chapter on the Parable of the Wheat and the Tares. This parable helps explain the story in Genesis and helps to better understand God's plan and solution to the Fall of Man and the Tree of Knowledge of Good and Evil.

I will look at a few examples like the parable of the Wheat and Tare, the parable of the Sheep and the Goat, and the parable of the Good Tree and the Bad Tree, and how they relate to the Tree of Knowledge and to show that there is Unity through Separation.

———————

In the Parable of the Wheat and Tares, Christ explains how paradise was corrupted by a thief in the night, and how evil was planted into the world. He also explains Gods love for us and the solution to the problem. Let's take a look at the parable in Matthew 13:24-30

"Another parable He put forth to them, saying: "The Kingdom of Heaven is like a man who sowed good seed in his field; but while men slept, his enemy came and sowed tares among the wheat, and went his way. But when the grain had sprouted and produced a crop, then the tares also appeared. So, the servants of the owner came and said to him, "Sir, did you not sow good seed in your field? How then does it have tares? He said to them, 'An enemy has done this, the servants said to him, 'Do you want us then to go and gather them up? But He said, 'No, lest while

you gather up the tares you also uproot the wheat with them. Let both grow together until harvest, and at the time of harvest I will say to the reapers, "First gather together the tares and bind them in bundles to burn them but gather the wheat into my barn."

Christ then explains the parable in Matthew 13:36-43 "Then He left the crowd and went into the house. His disciples came to him and said, "Explain to us the parable of the weeds in the field." He answered, "The one who sowed the good seed is the Son of Man. This field is the world, and the good seed stands for the people of the kingdom. The weeds are the people of the evil one, and the enemy who sows them is the devil. The harvest is the end of the age, and the harvesters are angels. "As the weeds are pulled up and burned in the fire, so it will be at the end of the age. The Son of Man will send out his angels, and they will weed out of his kingdom everything that causes sin and all who do evil. They will throw them into the blazing furnace, where there will be weeping and gnashing of teeth. Then the righteous will shine like the sun in the kingdom of their Father. Whoever has ears, let them hear."

As you can see, evil was planted into God's paradise just like in the Garden of Eden. Adam and Eve now know what is good and evil and that the two must grow together but at harvest the two would be separated.

God did not abandon us or start over but saved us and gave us free will. Free will to choose good over evil, life over death, and salvation over judgement. The good seed grows into wheat and the bad seeds grow into weed and through free will and faith we choose to be the Wheat or the Tare.

We choose good over evil and we become like wheat to God, where He separates the wheat from the weeds, the good from the evil, the faithful from the faithless, and brings them together according to their faith and deeds. You could say this is God's way of weeding things out and refining the earth back to Paradise.

In the Parable of the sheep and the goats, Christ explains how He is the Good Shepherd and we are His sheep. He explains how a Good sheep herder can tell the difference between His sheep and other goats and how His sheep know His voice. Let's look at the parable and look at the differences between goats and sheep.

Matthew 25:31 "When the Son of Man comes in his glory, and all the angels with him, he will sit on his glorious throne. All the nations will be gathered before him, and he will separate the people one from another as a shepherd separates the sheep from the goats. He will put the sheep on his right and the goats on his left. "Then they will go away to eternal punishment, but the righteous to eternal life."

What is the difference between the sheep and the goat? Although they may look alike, they are very different, and it can be difficult to tell them apart. A good shepherd can tell the difference between them by their physical attributes and their behavioral characteristics.

Most goats have horns, but sheep do not. Goats have tails that point upwards and sheep have tails that hang down. Sheep and goats are separate species and cannot be interbred to produce fertile offspring.

Now, look at the behavior of the two. Sheep follow the sheep herder and depend on him. They tend to stay with the flock, and they are stronger together, they may go astray but the herder will bring them back. On the other hand, the goats follow nobody, and it goes its own way, the goatherds follow behind the goat. They tend to be alone and are aggressive towards others.

Goats will usually jump the fence and are defiant while sheep will stay in the fence and are obedient. The sheep follows and is dependent on the shepherd, the goat takes his own way and is independent, doing whatever he pleases not following the goatherd. Simply saying that "A sheep is led by its shepherd and a goatherd is led by his goat."

The sheep follows and is obedient while the goat is stubborn and arrogant. The sheep gets along with the flock while the goat is aggressive towards others. Just look at the differences between the two and ask yourself are you a goat or are you a sheep? The Shepherd knows all His sheep and will come to divide his sheep from the goats.

Christ is the Good Shepherd and He leads us to the Father. He gathers us together into one flock and we follow our Shepherd. He says "I know my Sheep and they know me" we are called His Sheep because we follow

Christ, our Good Shepherd, and He brings us back if we go astray.

We depend on Christ and are identified by Christ and when we follow in His ways, we become one of His Sheep. We are identified by our faith in Christ and by our characteristics that represent that faith.

We follow the ways of Christ as sheep who follow their shepherd, we depend on the salvation and redemption of Christ, and we have the attributes of the sheep; being humble, obedient, working well with others, and not going astray but staying close to the flock and our Good Shepherd.

When we are identified by Christ then we are known as His Sheep and are separated from the goats, for the goats are the unbelievers who go in their own way and are not dependent upon Christ, they live their lives like the goats and are stubborn and defiant to the ways of God, not following Christ who is The Way but going in their own way looking for self-justification. This is the difference between the sheep and the goats, the believers and the non-believers, the goats on the left and the sheep on the right, that one is good and the other is evil, that the two will be separated, and the sheep will be united together as one flock.

As you can see the mixing of goats and sheep is like the wheat and the tares and the knowledge of good and evil, in how, the two are intertwined together but also must be separated. The sheep and the goat may look alike but we can see their behavioral characteristics are different.

Although the two may look alike they can be picked apart just like the wheat and tares. The sheep are like the wheat of God they are His seed and His offspring, and He will lead them to the store houses of Heaven.

In the Parable of the Good Tree and Bad Tree, Christ explains how you can tell a good tree from a bad tree if you just look at its fruit. He explains that if the fruit is rotten then the tree is bad and if the fruit is good then the tree is good, explaining that a good tree doesn't bear bad fruit nor does a bad tree bear good fruit.

The understanding of the parable is that you can tell what kind of tree, good or bad, by looking at its fruit. Understand, we are the tree and our thoughts, words, and deeds are our fruit. This means you can tell a lot about a person if you just watch how they think and what they say and do.

Like the saying goes "a bad apple doesn't fall far from the tree", if you observe a person's actions you will be able to see who they are because a person is identified by their actions.

Christ then explains how the two trees will be separated, for the bad tree is no good and does not bear good fruit and must be cut off. On the other hand, the good tree bears good fruit and is rooted in faith, this fruit is faith that produces good works.

Let's look at this parable in *Matthew 7:16* "*By their fruit you will recognize them. Do people pick grapes from thorn* bushes, or figs from thistles? Likewise, every good tree bears good fruit, but a bad tree bears bad fruit. A good tree cannot bear bad fruit, and a bad tree cannot bear good fruit. Every tree that does not bear good fruit is cut down and thrown into the fire. Thus, by their fruit you will recognize them."

Also, in Luke 6:43 Christ explains, "No good tree bears bad fruit, nor does a bad tree bear good fruit. Each tree is recognized by its own fruit. People do not pick figs from thorn bushes, or grapes from briers. A good man brings good things out of the good stored up in his heart, and an evil man brings evil things out the evil stored up in his heart. For the mouth speaks what the heart is full of. "Why do call me, 'Lord, Lord,' and do not do what I say? As for everyone who comes to me and hears my words and puts them into practice, I will show you what they are like."

    As you can see the tree is the root or source of the fruit. If the tree is good then it produces good fruit, if the tree is bad then it produces bad or rotten fruit. A good tree cannot bear bad fruit just as a bad tree cannot bear good fruit.

The tree is the heart of men and the fruit is our words and deeds. If a man is evil in his heart it will show in his actions, his actions will prove who he is. If a man is good in his heart, it will be proven by his actions. Therefore, it is said, "You will know them by their fruits" for you can tell if a person is bad or good if you just look at their actions.

As we can see we are identified by our words and actions, which proceed from our thoughts and rooted in our hearts. What we do and say shows a lot about who we are and how we are identified either as a good tree or bad tree. These two trees will be separated although they grow together now.

In Matthew 12:33 it says, 'Either make the tree good and its fruit good or make the tree bad and its fruit bad; for the tree is known by its fruit." You brood of vipers, how can you, being evil, speak what is good? For the mouth speaks out of that which fills the heart."

Matthew 3:10 "The axe is already laid at the root of the trees; therefore, every tree that does not bear good fruit is cut down and thrown into the fire."

Just as the sheep and the goats are separated, the wheat and the tares are separated, so as the good tree is separated from the bad tree. You can see now that although good and evil grow together they must be separated. The goats will be on the left, the tares thrown into the fire, and the bad tree will be cut down. On the other hand, the sheep will be on the right, the wheat stored in heaven, and the good tree will be rooted in Christ and will remain forever. As you can see, we are identified by our faith in God and our good fruit. That the Will of God is that we have faith and do good.

John 6:29 "Jesus answered, "The work of God is this: to believe in the one he has sent."

John 6:40 "For my Father's will is that everyone who looks to the Son and believes in him shall have eternal life, and I will raise them up at the last day."

Romans 12:1-2 "Do not be conformed to this world, but be transformed by the renewal of your mind, that by testing you may discern what is the will of God, what is good and acceptable and perfect."

1 Peter 3:11 "Turn away from evil and do good."

In Conclusion, there is unity through separation, which is the unification of Gods people and the separation from evil.

From the Garden of Eden where evil was planted into the minds of men through the tree of knowledge of Good and Evil, to the thief who planted bad seeds with good seeds in God's paradise, to the mixing and separating of the sheep and the goat, and to the good tree and the cutting down of the bad tree, you can see that good must be separated from evil although the two grow together.

Although there is good and evil in the world, we have free will to choose between the two and although they grow together, we must choose what we will be. You can see that we are identified by our faith and our works and this is how we are identified as His sheep, the wheat amongst tares, and the good tree that produces good fruit.

Chapter 8

Pairs by Equal Opposites

Everything in the natural world is made up in pairs by equal opposites to show the relationship between good and evil and the difference between the two. This relationship shows that good is always better than evil and that light overcomes the darkness.

However, in relation they reflect each other as a mirror would where one is seen from the other. This means one can't be seen without the other or by seeing what is bad we also see what is good, for good is the equal opposite of bad.

This is the knowledge of good and evil where we learn what is good from evil and we discern one from the other. This knowledge reveals that one is always greater than the other and one is always better than the other.

This shows the nature and glory of God; that God is good, God is light, God is love, God is righteousness, truth, and justice. Through this knowledge of pairs by equal opposites or duality we see the oneness of God and glory of God through Creation.

The natural world is seen in pairs by equal opposites. Pairs by equal opposites are defined as things that are paired but equally opposite, they are two extremes that oppose each other but are paired together.

For example, Good and Evil, Light and Darkness, Up and Down, Right and Wrong, Life and Death, Natural and Spiritual, everything is paired in this way.

Opposites oppose each other and go against each other. Opposites do not attract but rather like items do. Opposites dispel and repel against each other.

Opposites prove that one goes against the other, one is greater than the other, and one gives proof to the other. There is a misconception that the two create balance which stems from the understandings of the yin and yang.

Sources from tcmworld.com define yin and yang as "Everything contains yin and yang. They are two opposite yet complementary energies. What does this really mean? Although they are totally different--opposite--in their individual qualities and nature, they are interdependent. Yin and Yang cannot exist without the other; they are never separate. For example, night and day form a Yin-Yang pair. Night is Yin and day is Yang. Night looks and is very different than day, yet it is impossible to have one without the other. Both create a totality, a complete whole. This inseparable and interpenetrating relationship is reflected in the form of the Yin-Yang symbol. Nisarga Yoga states that "Yin and Yang complement one another. In the same way, the purpose on non-dual mindfulness isn't to eradicate duality. The purpose is to recognize that duality, or the appearance of separation, has an unconditional place within life, or undivided wholeness. The eradication of duality- if it were at all achievable- might cause a pure state of oneness, but this is still another extreme. Indeed, the concept of oneness would instantly perish without its counterpart "duality." Both are provisional concepts, and we should use them as such. So, true non-duality is even beyond oneness.

As you can see the ideas mentioned above refer to two opposites complementing each other in a contrary fashion but together create a whole or oneness where one cannot exist without the other.

For example, Night and Day, both create and make up a Day. They both oppose each other and are different in nature. Although you cannot see or appreciate the day without the darkness, the day is still better than the dark. The two are separable and one can exist without the other.

The source states, *"duality must be eradicated and what appears to be divided is whole. That you cannot have or appreciate oneness if you did not have duality but the key to balance or oneness is to separate duality."*

The key is to recognize the duality and separate it into a oneness. Which is the understanding that one is greater than the other and one always consumes the other, in the same way, the light is greater than darkness and the day fully consumes the night.

Although you need one to see or appreciate the other, one is always superior to the other, in the same way, you need bad to see what is good and you need rain to appreciate the sunshine. This knowledge and understanding helps us to see that good is always superior to evil and that light is always superior over darkness.

The two complementary but proportional elements do not balance each other but proportionally oppose each other in a complementary fashion. Some say that there is balance between good and evil, however, the truth is the balance is tilted to the majority side and the inferior gives proof to the superior.

Light is not balanced by darkness but instead light fully exposes darkness and overpowers the darkness. How can someone appreciate or understand light if there was no darkness? The darkness helps us to see and understand the light and after being in darkness helps us to appreciate the light. We begin to understand that light is better than darkness.

Although they are proportional which means the lesser the light more the darkness, and vice versa, the more the light then lesser the darkness. Eventually one will fully consume the other. For example, just think of a light in a dark room that has a dimmer on it. With the light off it is completely dark in the room but as you cut the light on the brightness of the light shines and overcomes the darkness. The dimmer switch proportions light to enter the room to become dimmer or brighter compared to the darkness in the room. With the light at its brightest there would be no darkness left in the room. This better illustrates how light and darkness are proportional to each other and how one fully consumes the other.

The same idea can be looked at between good and evil. How could we understand or appreciate what is good if we never knew what was bad? How could we truly appreciate joy without ever experiencing pain? How can you appreciate the sunshine without the rain?

Although we appreciate and see the good things in life by experiencing the bad things in life, we also learn that good is better than bad, joy better than pain, and the sunshine is better than the rain. Although both are needed to help appreciate and understand the other, one is always greater than its opposite.

Being exposed to evil we learn that there is no good in evil, that evil or bad things are just that, no good, and they give proof to the things that are good. We have knowledge of both good and evil and we learn that good is better than evil.

These are not balanced but opposing forces. The balance comes from you choosing right over wrong because choosing wrong over right would mean you are imbalanced.

The "Law of One" states that there is one God and none beside him. This law creates a oneness where we understand God is Good and God is Light which means God is One or also one sided. The understanding of oneness is to discern good between evil and separate the two by learning good from evil but also learning that good in its own nature is better than evil.

The natural world is created in pairs by equal opposites so that we learn the goodness of God and the difference between good and evil. We can look at many things in creation that show this relationship between yin and yang.

This relationship consists of the two opposites revealing their true nature by going against each other. You start to see them for what they truly are. One is always greater than the other and the other gives proof to the greater.

Let's go through some pairs of equal opposites to get a better idea of this relationship. Here are some pairs of equal opposites: Light and Dark, Day and Night, Good and Bad, Right and Wrong, Up and Down, Increase and Decrease, Life and Death, Spirit and Flesh, Order and Chaos, Positive and Negative, Arrogant and Modest, Punishment and Forgiveness, Love and Hate, Victory and Defeat, and I could go on and on.

The idea is to understand that these pairs are equally opposite and oppose each other and that one is always better than the other. This relationship displays the nature of what is good and the Glory of God.

The Glory of God is the knowledge that God is Good, God is Light, and God is Love. The knowledge that God despises evil and rewards what is good. The knowledge that God stands for what is good and is truth, righteousness, and peace. The knowledge that God calls us out of the darkness into his wonderful light. Finally, knowing that God is love and His love surpasses all evil.

In creation, after Adam and Eve ate from the tree of knowledge of Good and Evil and paradise was lost, the natural world became corrupted. Good was now mixed with evil and now we must separate the two and learn what is what.

This is explained further in the parable of the Wheat and the Tare. We have the two set before us and we must choose between Good and Evil, Life and Death, Right and Wrong. We must choose to be the wheat and not the tare.

There is no balance between the two only that they must be separated. One gives light to the other, one is greater than the other, and the other gives proof to the one. You can learn from the two and by the knowledge of good and evil you can wisely choose which one is better.

Some say these opposites attract as if they balance each other, but that is not true, the opposites oppose each other and balance each other in a complementary fashion.

Some say these two forces cancel each other out as if neither exist, but the truth is, one cancels the other out by being dominant. These complementary but opposite pairs are extreme opposites. They are complementary because they are contrasted against each other but the balance between the two is the dominant side.

The weaker side gives proof to the more dominant side by proving that the one is greater, stronger, and better than the other. There is always the side of the victor and the defeated, whereby, the victor is always victorious over the defeated. In the same way, good always prevails over evil and light over darkness.

Just like the idea of yin and yang there is another idea that is similar, which is karma. Karma is described as what goes around comes around and what goes up must come down. That every action has an equal reaction. It is equal and fair payment for any action. If you do wrong then you will be done wrong and if you do right then you will be done right, so that every action has an equal reaction.

Understanding there is rewards in good deeds and punishments in bad deeds. The Bible describes this as everyman receiving according to his deeds or "reaping what you sow". The Bible explains this as a person receiving exactly what he gives. If you sow good things you will reap good things, however, if you sow bad seeds you will reap bad fruit.

Karma is described as each person receiving what they deserve. Here we can see that unlike yin and yang and the balance between two items we see that karma is balanced by like items. Good begets good and bad begets bad. Good and bad are not equal or balanced but oppose each other and attract like items.

These opposing sides or extreme opposites do not balance each other out but instead one gives light to the other, one gives proof to the other, and one is greater than the other.

For example, think of the sun and the moon and how the sun is the greater light and the moon is the lesser light, in which, one rules the day and one rules the night. Together they give proof to each other because how could you appreciate the light without the darkness or expose the darkness without the light.

The idea is that light is greater than darkness and exposes the darkness for what it is and fully consumes it. The definition of light is the absence of darkness. This helps to better understand that good is the absence of evil and love is the absence of hate.

This helps us to appreciate that light prevails over darkness, just as, the day prevails over the night. Therefore, we understand that good prevails over evil. Karma explains how opposites don't attract or complement each other but that good rewards good and bad rewards bad.

These two things are separate and equally opposite but are in complementary pairs. Unlike yin and yang where the two create a balance between duality we see that karma shows how the two oppose each other and create oneness through separation.

 These pairs are opposites, but some say they are balanced because one can't exist without the other, but that is not true, one can exist without the other and one can exist alone or independent of the other.

The idea that you can't have one without the other doesn't mean they are balanced or co-dependent of each other but that they give proof to each other. It is better understood that one can't be seen without the other, one can't be appreciated without the other, and one can't be valued without the other. Understanding that one is seen through the other, one gives proof to the other, and one gives value through contrast.

This relationship between the two sheds light and gives contrast to better see and appreciate the greater and not the lesser. The truth is you can have one without the other, but you can't see or appreciate one without the other.

One always gives glory to the other, the weak gives proof to the strong, darkness gives proof to light, evil gives proof to good. At the same time this proof gives glory to the superior and not the inferior, proving that good is better evil and that light is superior to darkness.

One totally consumes the other, hence, in true light there is complete absence of darkness, which means light can exist alone and that light prevails over darkness. The darkness gives proof to the light, in that, we understand light is superior to darkness.

When viewed together one can help you see the other but when separated we are able to see they are in total opposition to each other and that only one remains, which is the better, greater, stronger, more positive, dominant side.

In Conclusion, pairs by equal opposites are not seen as equals but as opposites that are paired in complementary but contrasting fashion.

Have you ever heard the saying "The truth tells no lie" or "there is no lie in the truth"? We know that a lie is the opposite of telling the truth.

We understand that we would not know what a lie was without knowing the truth, we know the more you lie the less you are telling the truth. We see that the two are proportional to each other.

We know to lie is wrong and no one likes being lied to. In this instance, we appreciate truth and we see that telling the truth is better that telling a lie. We understand that we reap what we sow and that every good deed is rewarded with equal not opposite reactions.

In the same way, truth exposes the lie and we see that light exposes the darkness. There is no darkness found in true light and light is the absence of darkness. The light prevails over darkness, good prevails over evil, and truth prevails over lies.

It is what it is, and it is the nature of things created. God created things in pairs so that we may see the difference between the two. To understand light is light, good is good, and bad is bad, it is the nature of things itself. You cannot twist the nature of things and call what is good bad and what is bad good. We must see them for what they are and separate the two.

I will leave you with a popular saying and scripture. *A lie doesn't become truth, wrong doesn't become right, and evil doesn't become good, just because it's accepted by a majority.*

Isaiah 5:20 "Woe to those who call evil good and good evil, who put darkness for light and light for darkness, who put bitter for sweet and sweet for bitter!"

In the end, we can't twist the nature of things we must see them for what they truly are. That they are pairs but equally opposites.

Chapter 9

The Natural and Spiritual

There is an order to all things, there is a natural order and spiritual order, things seen and things unseen, each having their own nature and glory. We can look at this as the natural world and the spiritual world, things of the flesh and things of the spirit.

The natural world is nature and represents the earth and the spiritual world is spirit and represents heaven. The creation of earth is beautiful and full of purpose and life; however, its nature is temporary and perishable. We can see this as we look at nature and how the seasons go through cycles of life and death.

The spiritual world is spirit and represents heaven or spiritual things. The creation of heaven is the glorification of all things and its glory is everlasting and imperishable. If we look at things of heaven and the spirit, we can see how it represents eternal life.

We can see that each have their own order and their own glory, things that are of the earth and things that are of heaven, things that are seen and things unseen, things material and things of the spirit. I will examine the nature of these things, both the natural and the spiritual as to better understand their order and their glory.

In the Bible, 1 Corinthians 15:35-57 Paul discusses the resurrection of the body, the natural man, and the spiritual man, and I will base this chapter on this Bible verse.

"But someone will ask, "How are the dead raised? With what kind of body will they come? How foolish! What you sow does not come to life unless it dies. When you sow, you do not plant the body that will be, but just a seed, perhaps of wheat or of something else. But God gives it a body as he has determined, and to each kind of seed he gives its own body. Not all flesh is the same: People have one kind of flesh, animals have another, birds another and fish another. There are also heavenly bodies and there are earthly bodies; but the splendor of the heavenly bodies is one kind, and the splendor of the earthly bodies is another. The sun has one kind of splendor, the moon another and the stars another, and star differ from star in splendor."

"So, will it be with the resurrection of the dead. The body that is sown is perishable, it is raised imperishable; it is sown in dishonor, it is raised in glory; it is sown in weakness, it is raised in power; it is sown a natural body, it is raised a spiritual body."

"If there is a natural body, there is also a spiritual body. So, it is written: "The first man Adam became a living being, the last Adam became a life-giving spirit. The spiritual did not come first, but the natural, and after that the spiritual. The first man was of the dust of the earth; the second man is of heaven. As was the earthly man, so are those who are of the earth; and as is the heavenly *man, so also are those who are of heaven. And just as we have borne the image of the earthly man, so shall we bear the image of the heavenly man."*

I will examine this further and explain the natural order and the spiritual order, the natural body and the spiritual body, and how God has determined this in His design of Creation and the glorification of all things. I will look at things in nature like the caterpillar and the butterfly and how God puts signs in His Creation to show the relationship and difference between the natural world and the spiritual world.

The natural world is the physical or material world, which is described as things of the earth or earthly things. These things of the physical visible world are the natural order of things that was created by God as the Creation of the earth.

All the animals, the birds, the fish, all kinds of flesh, even the natural man have their own bodies. The physical world has an order or laws that it must follow which were determined by God. The way nature is designed, the way seeds are sowed, and plants are reaped, the way a seed grows into a beautiful flower, are all part of Gods design of the natural world.

However, the weakness in nature is that all things wither away and perish, soon that flower will reach its fullness and purpose and will die in the fall and winter. This is the glory of the natural world, that indeed there is purpose, life, and great design but in its weakness, things are temporary and perishable.

1 Peter 1:24 "For all flesh is as grass, and all the glory of man is as the flower of grass, the grass wither, and the flower there falls away."

The natural man is born into this world in the flesh, he is sown in the natural body which comes first. The natural body is corruptible, perishable, and mortal and will wither away and die. This the order of the natural world, in which, all things born of flesh will perish and die. So, we are born into this world as the natural man or the first man, and we live, grow, and enjoy life and the things of the earth, until the day our soul leaves this mortal body.

In the natural world, life thrives and continues to thrive through a cycle of reproduction of life and death. The earth in its own glory is beautiful and wonderfully made but also having an order that comes before heaven. God in His design determined that heaven would come after earth and the spiritual man would come after the natural man.

God glorified all things by showing that what is perishable will be made imperishable, what is mortal will be immortal, and what is temporary will be made eternal. God in His Glory shows that all things physical will be made spiritual and that what comes after the physical is the spiritual.

There is an order and design that proves the latter is better than the former, what is to come is better than what is passed away, and what is imperishable is better than the perishable.

―――――――――

The spiritual world is the metaphysical or immaterial world, which is described as things of heaven or heavenly things. These things or the unseen spiritual world is the spiritual order that was created by God as the Creation of the heavens.

All things in the sky or in the heavens, the sun, the moon, and the stars, even the spiritual man have their own bodies, splendor, and glory. The spiritual world has an order or laws that it must follow which were determined by God. The way the nature of heaven is designed, the way the planetary bodies move in their own set out paths, how the sun comes in the day and the moon comes in the night, how the stars live extremely long lives, are all part of the Creators grand design. He did this so that we look at things of the earth and things of heaven and can see the difference between the two.

The difference that one is weakness and the other is strength, one is dishonor and the other is glory, one is perishable and the other is imperishable. The strength and glory of the spiritual order are that all things are made new in Spirit and are made eternal and everlasting.

The verse says the spiritual man comes after the natural man and that something does not come to life unless it dies. Therefore, it is through death we are born into the spiritual world. There is the natural man which comes first and then which comes after the natural is the spiritual.

This is the second man, that which is born of heaven. The heavenly or spiritual body is incorruptible, imperishable, and immortal and will never die but will live forever. This is the order that God has determined for the Creation of the earth and the heavens and for the natural body and spiritual body.

It is determined that all things imperishable would come after the perishable, so that God would have Glory in all things. In a twinkling of an eye, we will all be changed and transformed at the day of Resurrection and be given our new spiritual bodies. Our souls whether dead or alive will be resurrected into the new immortal body.

Then, heaven will come down on earth, there will be a new heaven and new earth, where all things are being made new, and where the earth is being renewed and restored. This is the spiritual world or the glorified earth, heaven on earth, where we will live eternally as life giving spirits.

Think of the physical body and how in its great design it still gets tired, hungry, and thirsty. The natural body ages and gets old, gets aches and pains, and begins to break down over time. We know the order for this body is to have rest, food, and water. This body needs to be exercised and even at its best is still only temporary, eventually, the inevitable will occur.

Just imagine a better body, a spiritual body that in its design never gets tired, hungry, or thirsty. Imagine this body does not break down but is indestructible. Imagine a body that needs no rest, food or water, feels no more pain and no more sorrow, an everlasting body that lives eternally.

This is the joy God has stored for us that we cannot even begin to imagine. This is the glorification of the body from the natural born man to the resurrected spiritual man.

1 Peter 1:4-5 "God has something stored up for you in heaven, where it will never decay or be ruined or disappear. You have faith in God, whose power will protect you until the last day. Then he will save you, just as he has always planned to do."

1 Corinthians 2:9 "This is what the Scriptures mean when they say, "No eye has seen, no ear has heard, and no mind has imagined what God has prepared for those who love him."

    I will look at how the natural man and spiritual man are described to see the difference between the two. Both the natural man and spiritual man are inside us and are described as the carnal mind of man and the spiritual mind of God.

All men born of the flesh are carnal minded and have the ways of men, desiring things of the flesh and of this world. All men born of the spirit through Christ are spiritual minded and have the ways of God, desiring things of the Spirit and of heaven.

The earth is represented as the dust of the earth from which the natural man came from, and heaven is represented as the breath of life from which the spiritual man comes from. The natural man instinct is to do evil, however, the spiritual instinct is to do what is good and pleasing to God.

The carnal mind of a man is the sinful man who is impure and desires unrighteousness, this is the natural man who is born in sin through Adam. The natural carnal man does the desires of the flesh and is filled with wickedness; therefore, the natural body dies and perishes away because the flesh is in sin and the wages for sin is death.

The spiritual mind of God is the holy man who is pure and desires righteousness, this is the spiritual man who is born again through Christ, the second man. The spiritual godly man does the desires of the Spirit and is filled with the Spirit; therefore, the spiritual body is eternal and last forever because the Spirit is without sin, and through Christ death and resurrection He paid the wages for our sins. The spiritual man who comes after the natural sinful man no longer does the things of the flesh but strives to do the things of the Spirit.

Galatians 5:17 "For the flesh lust against the Spirit, and the Spirit against the flesh: and these are contrary to one another: so that you cannot do the things that you would."

The spiritual man is the man who desires to do the Will of God and to love His ways, which are Truth, Righteousness, Goodness, Justice, Peace, Love, and all the fruits of the Spirit, in which, these things are the things of heaven or the heavenly things and these desires are what make the spiritual man.

For flesh and blood will not inherit the kingdom of God, but the spiritual man through Christ will inherit the kingdom by faith. When Christ returns, He will resurrect the dead in Christ and the ones who are alive, in a twinkling of an eye to our new spiritual bodies, that will be purged of sin and perfected through the Spirit.

There will be no remembrance of sin for sin will be no more, for the former things are passing away and a new heaven and a new earth are being made, for all things are being glorified by God through Christ.

Revelations 21:1 "Then I saw a "new heaven and a new earth, for the first heaven and the first earth had passed away, and there was no longer any sea. I saw the Holy City, the new Jerusalem, coming down out of heaven from God, prepared as a bride beautifully dressed for her husband."

Isiah 43:18 "Remember not the former things, nor consider the things of old. "Behold, I am doing a new thing; now it springs forth, do you not perceive it?"

Can you perceive how in nature the old is passing away and a new thing is being made? Look at the trees and the flowers and how they go through cycles of old and new. In the wintertime, they pass or wither away, but in the springtime new life springs forth!!! Can you perceive it? That this life is the former life which passes away and the eternal life after is what springs forth.

God has made all things new, and He has prepared for us a new perfected body and a new heaven and earth. All this was prepared since the beginning, it is all in His design, that what comes after is better than what is passing away. This design and creation display's how the natural man will put on the spiritual man, the mortal will put on immortality, and the perishable will become imperishable.

Ephesians 1:4-5 "Even as he chose us in him before the foundation of the world, that we should be holy and blameless before him. In love he predestined us for adoption as sons through Jesus Christ, according to the purpose of his will,"

If we look at nature and perceive what is around us, we can see that God has a message designed in nature to give glory to God in all things. How we can see this theme of before and after of how nature dies in the fall and is reborn in spring, how what is temporary comes before what is eternal, how what is perishable comes before what is imperishable?

Howbeit that it be this way! It is amazing to see the grand design that God had planned and prepared from the beginning.

For example, think of the caterpillar and the butterfly. Think of how the caterpillar lives its life in caterpillar form, crawling around the ground until the day it goes into its cocoon.

There the caterpillar rest and is transformed into a beautiful butterfly and flies away. Think of how the caterpillar crawls and is limited and bound to the earth, only being able to eat off leaves.

Now think of the butterfly and how it has wings and flies, not being limited to the ground but can fly into unknown parts never reached before, and how the butterfly eats the nectar of flowers instead of leaves.

This understanding helps us see the glory and transformation of the caterpillar into the butterfly.

I will examine how the caterpillar and butterfly show an interesting feature as to how the natural body is transformed into the spiritual body.

If you look at the caterpillar and the butterfly you will see the hand of God and how nature works. It is interesting to see the caterpillar transition and transform into the butterfly.

Some say this would represent life and maturity, like a flower blossoming and blooming, but it shows something far greater on the spiritual side.

As the life form of the caterpillar ends, it transforms into a new stage of life which is the butterfly. It shows us that this physical life on earth is the caterpillar and at the end of that life we transform into the next stage of life, which is the butterfly.

The cocoon represents death or rest and the transition into the next life. The bible says we are the natural man first then comes the spiritual man.

Just by looking at nature we can see that we are the physical man, caterpillars living and enjoying life on earth.

At the end of this life, we go into our rest and transformation and become reborn as the spiritual man, the butterfly, which is the glory of the caterpillar.

In Conclusion, Paul is preaching the Gospel of Christ and the resurrection of the dead. He is stating that his message is not in vain for Christ indeed resurrected from the dead, He was the first fruits being the first resurrected unto life, that there were 500 witnesses some who were alive and some who have fallen asleep that witnessed the resurrected body of Christ.

This is the message that Paul is preaching, that indeed, the dead will be resurrected in Christ. He then explains the glory of the body and that each body has its own glory, just as earthly bodies have one splendor, heavenly bodies have their own splendor.

So, he says the resurrection is like this: the natural body and the spiritual body; one is perishable, corruptible, and mortal, the other which comes after is imperishable, incorruptible, and immortal.

That what is sown is not what is raised up! It is sown a natural body and it is raised up a spiritual body. But someone will ask "How are the dead raised? With what kind of body will they come?" How foolish! What you sow does not come to life unless it dies.

If there is a natural body, there is also a spiritual body. The spiritual did not come first, but the natural, and after that the spiritual. The first man was from the dust of the earth, the second man is of heaven. For flesh and blood cannot inherit the Kingdom of God, nor does the perishable inherit the imperishable. For at the last trumpet, we will be changed in the twinkling of an eye, raised up to our eternal bodies.

We are all first born in the physical and are born in sin and death through Adam the first man; however, we are reborn in the Spirit and freed from sin and death and have eternal life through Christ. For if any man be in Christ, has he not resurrected from the dead and become alive? When we are baptized, we die with Christ and are resurrected to life, this is the first resurrection, the second death have no power over them.

The first death is physical and inevitable, for all flesh or what is perishable will perish. For as dust we are, dust we will return, and the Spirit will go back to where it came from. This is the spiritual life which comes after the natural death, which is, to be absent from the body is to be in the presence of the Lord.

When we leave our bodies, our soul will be in the spiritual state or disembodied state where we rest and reside in

Paradise, which is, a temporary heaven until Christ returns to resurrect us to our new spiritual bodies and brings heaven on earth, which is, the new earth and new heaven.

Therefore, it is amazing to see that what was not first was spiritual, but that which is natural; and afterward that which is spiritual. It is interesting because it makes sense that what is imperishable come after what is perishable and that all things are being renewed through Christ by God.

Yes, indeed, we are to appreciate the natural and all God's Creation but also understand that the natural has its flaws and is not perfect, understanding that we get old and die, and that the natural is sowed in dishonor and weakness.

However, the spiritual, which is better than the natural, comes after the natural body and is the spiritual body, a body that doesn't get old and die but lives forever, the spiritual, which is being perfected and raised in glory and strength.

I like to think of it as the glorification of the body. Just like the caterpillar to the butterfly we are transformed from the natural body to the spiritual body. What God has prepared for us is greater than what we can imagine. He has prepared for us a perfect body and a perfect earth.

All this was prepared since the beginning, it is all in His design, that what comes after is better than what is passing away. It is the glorification of all things through Christ, so that all Glory be to God.

I can only imagine or have a glimpse as to what God has prepared for us by looking at nature and understanding the natural order and spiritual order of things, and then I can begin to have faith in the great things to come.

1 Corinthians 2:9 "No eye has seen, no ear has heard, no mind conceived what God has prepared for those who love him."

Chapter 10

The Battle between Spirit and Flesh

The whole Bible can be summed up in this battle between good and evil, the battle between God and the devil, the battle between light and darkness, and the battle between the spirit and the flesh.

We know that Satan rebelled against God and is the father of lies and rebellion. He stands against all that is Holy and Good and is opposed to God. We know the devil roams around like a devouring lion tempting people to disobey God and to follow him.

It is this battle between God and the devil which is a fight for your mind, body, and soul. Therefore, we are to love God with all our mind, heart, and soul. We do this by loving God and obeying and living in His ways. It is this fight between light and darkness, a fight between good and evil, right and wrong, righteousness and wickedness that are defined as the Spirit and the Flesh.

Not only is the battle between good and evil understood as the overall context of the Bible, the whole story of how God defeats the devil and how good prevails over evil, is the overall understanding. This battle is not only in the spiritual realm but is also within. This battle is known as the battle between the Spirit and the flesh.

I will investigate how the Spirit and the flesh are at war with each other just as good and evil are at war with each other. We are in the middle of that war and we must choose which side we will stand for and fight against.

I stand for what is good and I stand for God, I choose good over evil, I choose the spirit over the flesh. Therefore, we are to put on the Armor of God for we are at battle between the Spirit and the flesh and the battle between good and evil.

Ephesians 6:12 "For we wrestle not against flesh and blood, but between principalities and rulers of darkness of this world, and against evil and spiritual wickedness in high places."

All humanity is now involved in a great controversy between Christ and Satan regarding the character of God, His law, and His sovereignty over the universe. This conflict originated in heaven when a created being, endowed with freedom of choice, in self-exaltation became Satan, God's adversary, and led into rebellion a portion of the angels. He introduced the spirit of rebellion into this world when he led Adam and Eve into sin. This human sin resulted in the distortion of the image of God in humanity, the disordering of the created world, and its eventual devastation at the time of the worldwide flood. Observed by the whole creation, this world became the arena of the universal conflict, out of which the God of love will ultimately be vindicated. To assist His people in this controversy, Christ sends the Holy Spirit and the loyal angels to guide, protect, and sustain them in the way of salvation. (nadadventist.org)

In battle, there are two sides and there is the victor and the defeated. The battle is a fight between both sides to whoever gains a victory or is in control. In battle you have weaknesses and strengths, advantages and disadvantages, skills and armor that are consistent with battles.

The battle between the Spirit and flesh are at constant war with each other, the flesh is weakness and the spirit is strength, the flesh desires the sinful nature and the spirit desires the spiritual nature, these two desires are contrary to each other and go against each other.

The flesh is the natural man or the sinful man, it is weak to fleshly or worldly desires, it is the carnal mind of man that desires to satisfy the flesh. The spirit is the spiritual man or the holy man, it is strong against fleshly desires and desires things of the spirit, it is the spiritual mind of God that desires to satisfy the spirit.

These two are against each other and are at war within your mind and body as well as in the world. It is the battle between good and evil and the battle between the spirit and the flesh.

The flesh is weak to sinful desires and physical temptations, it is a natural instinct in some cases to lie, cheat, act greedy or selfish at times. This is the nature of the flesh, it is selfish and produces things like jealousy, greed, envy, hate, arrogance, and pride. This nature is sinful and leads to things like lying, cheating, stealing, and unlawfulness which leads to death.

This is the nature of the spirit, it is selfless and produces things like love, kindness, humbleness, modesty, charity, and compassion. The nature of the spirit is spiritual and leads to things like honesty, integrity, loyalty, obedience, and faithfulness which leads to life.

The nature of the flesh is to sin, the nature of the Spirit is to do the Will of God. The desires of the flesh and the will of the Spirit are contrary to one another. The carnal mind desires to satisfy the works of the flesh while the spiritual mind of God desires to satisfy the fruits of the Spirit.

Let us observe some scriptures that give truth and understanding about the battle between the flesh and the Spirit.

Romans 8:5-9 For those who are according to the flesh set their minds on the things of the flesh, but those who are according to the Spirit, the things of the Spirit. For the mind is set on the flesh is death, but the mind set on the Spirit is life and peace, because the mind set on the flesh is hostile toward God; for it does not subject itself to the law of God, for it is not even able to do so.

Ephesians 2:3 Among them we too all formerly lived in the lusts of our flesh, indulging the desires of the flesh and of the mind, and were by nature children of wrath, even as the rest.

Romans 13:14 But put on the Lord Jesus Christ and make no provision for the flesh regarding its lust.

1 Timothy 6:11-12 But you, man of God, flee from all this, and pursue righteousness, godliness, faith, love, endurance and gentleness. Fight the good fight of faith. Take hold of the eternal life to which you were called when you made your good confession in the presence of many witnesses.

Galatians 5:17 For the flesh lust against the Spirit, and the Spirit against the flesh: and these are contrary to each other: so that you cannot do the things that you would. For the flesh sets its desires against the Spirit, and the Spirit against the flesh; for these are in opposition to one another, so that you may not do the things that you please.

Romans 13:14 but put on the Lord Jesus Christ and make no provision for the flesh regarding its lusts.

Galatians 5:24 Now those who belong to Christ Jesus have crucified the flesh with its passions and desires.

Galatians 5:18-23 But if you are led by the Spirit, you are not under the law. Now the deeds of the flesh are evident, which are: immorality, impurity, sensuality, idolatry, sorcery, enmities, strife, jealousy, outbursts of anger, disputes, dissensions, factions, envying, drunkenness, carousing, and things like these, of which I forewarn you, that those who practice such things will not inherit the kingdom of God.

Galatians 5:22-23 But the fruit of the Spirit is love, joy, peace, patience, kindness, goodness, faithfulness, gentleness and self-control. Against such things there is no law.

2 Timothy 3:16-17 All Scripture is God-breathed and is useful for teaching, rebuking, correcting and training in righteousness, so that the servant of God may be thoroughly equipped for every good work.

Sources say, we all face the struggle of dealing with our flesh. Paul said, *"For the mind set on the flesh is death, but the mind set on the Spirit is life and peace, because the mind set on the flesh is hostile toward God.* We all have a flesh and it does not magically vanish when a person becomes a believer. Jesus said, *"The spirit is willing, but the flesh is weak."* The flesh is our old, carnal nature. It must be dealt with. Think of it as the weak-willed man within us. Our fallen nature has a side to it that has no character, no resolve, no backbone, and no self-control. The Bible says that the flesh is a slave to impurity and lasciviousness, serves the law of sin, has passions and desires, brings corruption, has its own wisdom, wages war against the soul and has nothing good in it. It is the flesh that desires and generates immorality, impurity, sensuality, idolatry, sorcery, enmities, strife, jealousy, outbursts of anger, disputes, dissensions, factions, envying, drunkenness, and carousing. It is the weak-willed man inside us. When we speak of flesh, or the carnal nature, keep in mind that we are primarily referring to a mind-set, a way of thinking. It is the insanity which keeps us bound up in sin that we know is destroying us. However, if you want to overcome habitual sin, you must learn to walk in the Spirit. This process is a lifelong daily battle. After telling his readers to walk in the Spirit, Paul goes on to say, *"For the flesh sets its desires against the Spirit, and the Spirit against the flesh; for these are in opposition to one another, so that you may not do the things that you please".* In this verse, we see the daily battle raging inside every believer who wants to please God and yet finds that part of him simply wants to indulge in pleasure and sin.

Pure life ministries write, "This is where the typical Christian gets bogged down and discouraged. It seems that change will never come, that they are bound to live in defeat. This is not God's desire for His children. While it is true that one aspect of the spirit vs flesh war occurs in our daily lives, equally true is that the person who strives after righteousness, struggles against the desires of the flesh, and pursues a course of holiness, gradually gains ground in the contest. This process takes time and requires the believer to diligently cooperate with the Holy Spirit's work. The sincere seeker soon discovers a previously unknown strength forming within him. He will notice that temptations no longer grip him with overwhelming power not present early on in his faith to overcome temptation. Before long, this man will come to know what it means to become a mature saint: to truly walk in the Spirit. This spiritual growth and development are not automatic. A person does not mature into godliness simply because his salvation experience happened a long time ago. He grows into the likeness of Christ only by daily cooperating with God's work in his inner man.

The struggle or the wrestling we experience in this battle is from the constant war going on inside us. We are in the flesh and we are spiritual. It is a part of our nature and the knowledge between good and evil. Therefore, we have weaknesses and we need the strength of God to keep us fighting. With the Spirit of God, we can conquer and overcome any weakness but where I am weak, He is made strong, God is my strength even in my times of weakness.

Therefore, we must put on the full Armor of God to protect us from temptations of the flesh. To give us victory over the flesh and help us to win this battle within. That although I may fall weak it is God who picks me up and forgives me, it is His Mercy and Love that keeps me lifted. It is His Spirit that comforts me and makes me strong, guides me in all truth and shows me how to seek His ways. This is how the spirit is made strong and can overcome the flesh.

Let's look at that Armor of God and see how it protects us in this battle between spirit and flesh.

Ephesians 6:10 Finally, be strong in the Lord and in his mighty power. Put on the full armor of God, so that you can take your stand against the devil's schemes. For our struggle is not against flesh and blood, but against the rulers, against the authorities, against the powers of this dark world and against the spiritual forces of evil in the heavenly realms. Therefore, put on the full armor of God, so that when the day of evil comes, you may be able to stand your ground, and after you have done everything to stand. Stand firm then, with the belt of truth buckled around your waist, with the breastplate of righteousness in place, and with your feet fitted with the readiness that comes from the gospel of peace. In addition to all this, take up the shield of faith, with which you can extinguish all the flaming arrows of the evil one. Take the helmet of salvation and the sword of the Spirit, which is the word of God.

Suit up in the full Armor of God: Sword of the Spirit, Shield of Faith, Breastplate of Righteousness, Helmet of Salvation, Belt of Truth and Boots of Peace.

The Sword of the Spirit, which is the Word of God, cuts through lies and deception. The Shield of Faith which is our Faith in Christ protects us. Our hearts are covered by the Breastplate of Righteousness and our minds guarded with the Helmet of Salvation. Strapped tight and grounded firmly in Truth, walking and preaching the Gospel of Peace.

The full armor protects us from the attacks and deception that Satan uses through the world; the world will persecute you, ridicule you, make you doubt your faith, make you question his word and will lead you astray, leading you to more sin and condemnation taking you further away from grace.

That is why we wear the Helmet of Salvation; this is knowing we are saved by God's Grace. We wear the

Breastplate of Righteousness, which is the Righteousness of God, which is Christ, and that we protect our hearts with righteousness. The Sword of the Spirit cuts through lies, deception, and confusion that may be thrown at us from the enemy. Preaching peace with the Boots of Peace and walking in it, having Faith as our shield to defend against the unfaithful and the wicked, and to be grounded in Truth wrapped around us as a belt.

The battle is not between flesh and blood but against unseen powers of darkness. The fight is for your soul, we have already been purchased by faith through Jesus Christ and we know how-to live-in Christ. We are His and nobody can snatch them out His Father's hand.

Satan's attacks will be for your mind, body and soul, he will try to get you to stop believing, start feeling guilty, he will get you to practice sin more and love what is wrong. These are the temptations and wiles of the devil.

This is what we are fighting spiritually in the flesh, each one of us, fighting the Good Fight and that the faith and goodness in us prevails through the power of the Spirit and Truth.

By faith in Christ's death and resurrection, the godly man has declared Jesus the Lord of his life, and his heart is set toward obedience. With God's Spirit inside him, the godly man can understand the deep things of the Spirit. He begins to see life differently. Life is no longer about pleasing himself but about pleasing his Lord.

The godly man knows he will still stumble as he strives toward holiness, but his goal is to be holy as His Lord is holy. He learns early that his fleshly attempts at holiness only result in pride and failure. The godly man learns that, as he surrenders his will to the Holy Spirit and relies upon Him for strength to overcome temptation and accomplish greater eternal goals than he ever thought possible.

A godly man is one who has died to his flesh. This does not mean he no longer faces temptation. It means that, when he is tempted, the decision about whether to give in has already been made. He relies on the power of the Holy Spirit to help him say "no" to his flesh and "yes" to the Spirit.

As he regularly opposes sin, he finds that his spirit grows stronger and temptation becomes easier to resist. A godly man is not a perfect man. We will never reach perfection until we are in the physical presence of Jesus. But the godly man embraces his manhood and knows that Jesus, not the world, has set the standard for what it means to be a real man. So, he strives daily to model his life after Jesus. He does not excuse sins and weaknesses he finds in himself but continually surrenders those areas to God and asks for His help in overcoming them. Regardless of physical appearance, social status, or economic standing, any man can be a godly man if he loves God with all his heart and seeks to obey Him in every area of his life.

───────────

What does it mean to walk in the Spirit? Believers have the indwelling Spirit of Christ, the Comforter who proceeds from the Father. The Holy Spirit assists believers in prayer and intercedes for God's people in accordance with the Will of God.

He also leads the believer into righteousness and produces His fruit in those that yielded to Him. Believers are to submit to the will of God and walk in the Spirit. A "walk" in the Bible is often a metaphor for practical daily living. The Christian life is a journey, and we are to walk it, we are to make consistent forward progress.

The biblical norm for all believers is that they walk in the Spirit: "If we live in the Spirit, let us also walk in the Spirit." In other words, the Spirit gave us life in the new birth, and we must continue to live, day by day, in the Spirit. To walk in the Spirit means that we yield to His control, we follow His lead, and we allow Him to exert His influence over us. To walk in the Spirit is the opposite of resisting Him or grieving Him.

Those who walk in the Spirit are united with Him and the bearers of the fruit the Spirit produces. Thus, those who walk in the Spirit walk in love--they live in love for God and for their fellow man. Those who walk in the Spirit walk in joy--they exhibit gladness in what God has done, is doing, and will do.

Those who walk in the Spirit walk in peace--they live worry-free and refuse anxiety. Those who walk in the Spirit walk in patience--they are known for having a "long fuse" and do not lose their temper.

Those who walk in the Spirit walk in kindness--they show tender concern for the needs of others. Those who walk in the Spirit walk in goodness--their actions reflect virtue and holiness.

Those who walk in the Spirit walk in faithfulness--they are steadfast in their trust of God and His Word. Those who walk in the Spirit walk in gentleness--their lives are characterized by humility, grace, and thankfulness to God.

Those who walk in the Spirit walk in self-control--they display moderation, constraint, and the ability to say "no" to the flesh.

Chapter 11

Fallen Angels and Idol gods

What are the fallen angels? They are Lucifer and his angels who rebelled against God and were cast out of heaven into the earth.

Revelations 12:7-9 states, "And there was war in heaven: Michael and his angels fought against the dragon; and the dragon fought and his angels and prevailed not; neither was their place found any more in heaven. And the great dragon was cast out, that old serpent, called the Devil, and Satan, which deceives the whole world: he was cast out into the earth, and his angels were cast out with him."

These angels who were cast out of heaven are the fallen angels who rebelled against God. Satan, who was Lucifer, was a beautiful and powerful angel of God, who rebelled against God and desired to be worshiped like God. He was a created being that was perfect in his ways until iniquity was found in him. This iniquity was his pride, like they say, "Pride comes before the Fall".

In Ezekiel 28:17 it states, "Your heart became proud on account of your beauty, and you corrupted your wisdom because of your splendor."

Lucifer became so impressed with his own beauty, intelligence, power, and position that he began to desire for himself the honor and glory that belonged to God alone. He let greed, envy, and jealousy make him want to exalt himself above God.

Isaiah 14:13 states, "For you have said in your heart: "I will ascend into heaven, I will exalt my throne above the stars of God; I will ascend above the height of the clouds, I will be like the Most High. "Yet you shall be brought down to Sheol, to the lowest depths of the Pit."

He left his place or position in the heavens to exalt himself above God and was thrown down to the lowest parts of the earth. He lost his power, beauty, and splendor and became the lowest and ugliest of creatures. In Genesis, after the fall of man, in the garden of Eden, Satan was cursed to the ground to walk on his belly and eat the dust of the earth.

Genesis 3:14 states, "So the LORD God said to the serpent, "Because you have done this, "Cursed are you above all livestock and all wild animals! You will crawl on your belly and you will eat dust all the days of your life."

Jesus describes in Luke that He saw Satan fall from heaven like lightning and that he has no power. He says that we have power over him and that he cannot harm us.

Luke 10:18-19 "He replied, "I saw Satan fall like lightning from heaven. I have given you authority to trample on snakes and scorpions and to overcome all the power of the enemy: and nothing shall by any means hurt you."

He has no power over man and man has power over him because he was made lower than man in the form of a serpent. He knows he lost his power, so he tempts men to rebel and go against God by disguising himself as an angel of light, therefore, hiding his true nature to deceive all men by sharing with them knowledge that is forbidden.

2 Corinthians 11:14 *"And no wonder, for even Satan disguises himself as an angel of light."*

The forbidden knowledge was knowing what was good and evil. Before eating from the Tree of Knowledge of Good and Evil, man only knew what was good. This knowledge of good and evil along with Free Will gave man a choice, to choose to do good and serve God, or follow Satan and do evil. To disobey and rebel against God, which is sin, or to serve God and follow in His ways, which is obedience.

Therefore, he is the adversary of God because he is in opposition to God. He has no power over men other than to tempt and to deceive, therefore, he is the tempter of temptations and the Great Deceiver. He leads men astray and takes them down the wrong path which includes idol worship, in which, he desires to intercept the true worship to the One and Only True God by doing what God does not like, which is idolatry.

As a result of him rebelling against God and exalting himself, Lucifer was cast out of heaven, he became corrupt and his name changed from Lucifer meaning "morning star" to Satan meaning "adversary". The angels who followed Satan is said to be a third of the angels in heaven that where cast to the earth. The Bible describes these fallen angels as stars.

Isiah 14:12 "How you have fallen from heaven, O shining star, son of the morning! You have been cast down to the earth, you who once laid low the nations."

Revelations 12:4 The Dragon and "Its tail swept away one-third of the stars in the sky, and he threw them to the earth."

Since, Satan the Dragon is referred to as a star, which fell or was cast from heaven, and Revelations says one-third of the stars were cast out with him, therefore, the stars are being referred to as the fallen angels. The fallen angels then came to the earth and desired the worship of men that is rightfully Gods.

What are idols or idolatry? Idolatry is the worship of idols, which are false gods, who are worshipped by people in the form of anything that is made by hands that represent these false gods or fallen angels. An idol can be anything made of stone, wood, or metal for the purpose of worship.

Isiah 2:8 states, "Their land has also been filled with idols; They worship the work of their hands, that which their fingers have made."

Psalm 135:15-18 "The idols of the nations are silver and gold, made by human hands. They have mouths, but cannot speak, eyes, but cannot see. They have ears, but cannot hear, nor is there breath in their mouths. Those who make them will be like them, and so will all who trust in them."

The idols described here are statues or images that cannot speak although they have mouths, they have form but no life in them, and can do nothing for you.

Isiah 45:20 "Ignorant are those who carry about idols of wood, who pray to gods that cannot save them."

Deuteronomy 4:15-19 "You saw no form of any kind the day the Lord spoke to you at Horeb out of the fire. Therefore, watch yourselves very carefully, so that you do not become corrupt and make for yourselves and idol, an image of any shape, whether formed like a man or a woman, or like any animal on the earth or any kind of bird that flies in the air, or like any creature that moves along the ground or any fish in the waters below. And when you look up to the sky and see the sun, the moon and the stars- all the heavenly array- do not be enticed into bowing down to them and worshipping things the Lord your God has apportioned to all the nations under heaven."

God is a Spirit and He is to be worshipped in Spirit and in Truth. For He Created all things and we worship the Creator, not the creation. God is the only one who rightly deserves our worship for He is our Creator. He Created the Heavens and the Earth and all things in it, He Created man and woman, and He Created the Angels.

For this reason, we do not bow down to an idol that we create with our hands, or anything God Created in the Heavens or Earth or beneath. We only worship the Creator, who is Sovereign over all creation, and who is to be worshiped in Spirit and Truth.

Romans 1:25 "They traded the truth about God for a lie. So, they worshipped and served the things God created instead of the Creator himself, who is worthy of eternal praise! Amen."

We are to worship the Creator not creation. In the Bible, God gives the Commandment against idolatry.

Exodus 20:3-5 "You shall have no other gods before me. You shall not make for yourself an image in the form of anything in heaven above or on the earth beneath or in the waters below. You shall not bow down to them or worship them; for I, the LORD your God, am a jealous God,"

2 Kings 17:12 "They served idols, concerning which the LORD had said to them, "You shall not do this thing."

God seen that they served idols so He gave them over to a reprobate mind, whereby, doing things they should not do.

Acts 7:42 "Then God turned away from them and gave them over to the worship of the sun, moon, and stars. This agrees with the book of prophets: "Was it me you were bringing sacrifices and offerings during those forty years in the wilderness, Israel?"

They were not sacrificing to God but were sacrificing to the golden calf of the Canaanites, which was an idol god, named Moloch or Baal. Satan and his angels desire to be worshipped as gods in the earth and they do so in the form of idols, which include, the Sun, Moon, and Stars.

They want to provoke God by teaching men evil and taking away worship to the One True God, whereby, teaching men to make and worship idols. These fallen angels or demons want men to worship them as stars in the forms of idols.

This is where pagan worship of nature comes in. The pagan worship of the sun and the moon and stars, which are also known as planets. These are considered idols or false gods and where they originate from.

I will look further into how Satan and his fallen angels were made into these false idol gods. How men who saw these fallen angels mistaken them for gods. How men made idols of them and personified them with nature as sun gods and moon goddesses. How in each culture from Sumerian, Egyptian, Babylonian, Greek, and Roman civilizations, there can be found traces of these false gods and their idols.

In the Bible, it describes how these angels fell from heaven and how they desired the women of the earth. That they came down to mate with the women of the earth and the women bore children, called Nephilim, which were Giants in the earth.

These fallen angels taught men all kinds of sorcery and abominations that is despised by God. When God had seen this and all the wickedness of the earth, which was filled with blood from all the evil in the earth. God had flooded the earth with water and destroyed everything in it, except the elect from God, which we know as Noah and his family.

Genesis 6-8 "Now it came to pass, when men began to multiply on the face of the earth, and daughters were born to them, the sons of God "fallen angels" saw the daughters of men, that they were beautiful; and they took wives for themselves of all whom they chose. There were giants on the earth in those days, and afterwards, when the sons of God came into the daughters of men and they bore children to them. These were the mighty men of old, men of renown. And God saw that the wickedness of man was great in the earth, and every imagination of the thoughts of his heart was only evil continually. And it repented the Lord that he had made man on the earth, and it grieved him at his heart. And the LORD said, I will destroy man whom I have created from the face of the earth; for I repent that I have made them. But Noah found grace in the eyes of the Lord."

The Book of Enoch speaks of a group of fallen angels who came down and shared ancient knowledge with humans, known as the Watchers.

"And they were in all two hundred fallen angels, who descended in the days of Jared on the summit of Mount Hermon. And the angels, the children of the heaven, saw and lusted after them, and said to one another: "Come, let us choose wives from among the children of men and beget us children." When the angels descended upon the earth, they started offering gifts of knowledge to both mortal men and women, thus defying the will of the

Creator. In exchange, the angels demanded respect and adoration. "And all the other together with them took unto themselves wives, and each chose for himself one, and they began to go unto them and to defile themselves with them, and they taught them charms and enchantments, and the cutting of roots, and they became pregnant and they bare great giants. "And Azazel taught men to make swords, and knives, and breastplates, and made known to them the metals of the earth and the art of working them. "And there arose much godlessness, and they committed fornication, and they were led astray, and became corrupt in all their ways. "And destroy all the spirits of the reprobate and the children of the Watchers because they have wronged mankind. Destroy all wrong from the face of the earth and let every evil work come to an end; and let the plant of righteousness and truth appear:"

These fallen angels, the watchers, who came down and taught men forbidden knowledge and bore children with the women, known as Nephilim, where the gods of old and were the false idol gods that were being worshipped in the earth before the Flood and also destroyed in the Great Flood. The earliest civilizations around the time of the flood were the Sumerians and the Egyptians.

In Sumerian religion they speak of the Shining Ones who came down on Mount Hermon in the land of Shinar. The land of Shinar translates to "land of the shining ones" also translated as "the fallen ones" or "shining ones".

These are the fallen angels who came down from heaven and taught men mystery knowledge.

Remember that they disguise themselves as angels of light and that they came down on Mount Hermon and taught men forbidden knowledge as in the Bible. Shinar is in ancient Sumer, later known as Babylon, and the Sumerians mistaken these shining ones or fallen angels to be gods and began to worship them in the form of idols, which are the sun, moon and star gods.

The Sumerian Sun god was Utu and the moon god was Nanna, along with many other star gods personified as elements of nature. The major deities in the Sumerian pantheon included: An, the god of the heavens, Enlil, the god of wind, Enki, the god of water and human culture.

These civilizations left behind many artifacts and remains of the old ancient gods that were worshipped in the earth before the flood. The Ancient gods of Old that many civilizations idolized where the fallen angels and Satan. The people who saw the angels fall from heaven thought they were gods, and these fallen angels came to men and taught them things like astrology, war, magic, sorcery, mysteries of the cosmos, and other things that were not to be shared with man.

These people in ancient civilizations before the flood, like Sumerian and Egyptian cultures, worshipped these fallen angels as gods. These false gods or idol gods desired to be worshipped and made them sacrifice children to the gods, in which, the people made idols of these entities.

This is where idol worship begins and the worship of false gods or many gods. These fallen angels of the earth are now personified and idolized in different cultures and pagan religions throughout time. They represent the polytheistic pagan gods of Babylon, Egypt, Greece, and Rome.

The pantheon of false gods, idol gods, and the fallen angels are repackaged over time into different cultures. The different ancient civilizations that worshipped these false gods before the flood and after are still present today. These false gods were made into idols; stone statues or carved wooden figurines.

This is what is considered idol worship and what they did not realize is what they saw fall from heaven, were not gods, but the fallen angels and Satan, who came to the earth to deceive all men into worshipping him. These false gods or idol gods are then shared and experienced by surrounding cultures like the Egyptians, the Babylonians, and then later transitions over into pagan Greek and Roman mythology.

This mystery or forbidden knowledge received in Sumer was recorded by a man named, Hermes Trismegistus, who wrote the Emerald Tablets of Thoth. He spread this mystery knowledge to the Egyptians which later spread to Greece.

Hermes (Greek god) who is also known as Thoth (Egyptian god) taught the mystery schools in Egypt and taught things like magic, alchemy, and sorcery, which is also known as Hermetics.

Source states, *"Hermes is placed, according to mythology, in the early days of the oldest dynasties of Egypt, long before the days of Moses. Some regard him as a contemporary of Abraham."-*

This places him around the time of the Sumerians and Egyptians and the time of Abraham. This makes perfect sense and aligns with all other references, in which, the knowledge he received was from the fallen ones or shining ones on Mount Hermon, which gives him the name Hermes, who is the father of Hermeticism.

He is said to have been the one person who brought this Hermetic knowledge from Sumer to Egypt. This is where we begin to see a trend and similarity of the many gods of Sumerian, Egyptian, Babylonian, Greek, and Roman cultures, in the forms of sun, moon, and star worship.

In Egypt, they practiced Hermetics and were taught by Hermes or Thoth in the mystery school knowledge. The same mystery teachings of Sumer in the land of Shinar on Mount Hermon were being inducted by the Egyptians.

In Egypt, they worshipped many gods that were very similar to the Sumerian gods. In Egypt, the Sun god was Ra and the Moon god was Khonsu, which is the same form of sun and moon worship of the Sumerian gods.

It is the same fallen angels with a different name according to their language and culture, also being attributed to forms of nature like the sun, the moon, and the elements. In the Egyptian pantheon of gods, you have the sun and wind god Amun-Ra, Isis the magic goddess, who is the wife of Osiris, the god of the dead, and mother of Horus, god of the sky, among many other gods.

There is a common theme among all these ancient cultures and practices, from Sumerians to Egyptians, and moving into Babylon, who takes all these cultures and create a new form of idol worship. I will look deeper into the Babylonian gods and how they coincide with the other cultures.

The Bible talks about Nimrod, the son of Cush, to be a mighty hunter who was the king of Babylon. Nimrod was angry with God for his ancestors being destroyed by the flood. He avenged himself against God and did all that he could to anger God.

He then built a tower, which is the tower of Babel, that he said would reach the heavens so that he could get to God out of anger, and to prevent from being flooded if another flood occurred.

He wanted to gather the people together to ascend into the heavens and wage war with God; now does not this sound closely familiar to Satan exalting himself above God and waging a war in heaven?

The name Nimrod means "the Rebel" or "to Rebel" as he wanted to defy God and build a tower so high out of arrogance. When God seen this and seen the anger aroused in him and the people, just like how He cast down

Satan, he destroyed and cast down that tower, and scattered the people in confusion by changing their language.

As these people left Babylon according to their language of people, they took with them the practices of Babylon.

Genesis 10:8 "And Cush begat Nimrod: he began to be a mighty one in the earth. 10 And the beginning of his Kingdom was Babel, and Erech, Accad, and Calneh, in the land of Shinar."

Genesis 11:1-9 "Now the whole world had one language and a common speech. As people moved eastward, they found a plain in Shinar and settled there. They said to each other, "Come, let's make bricks and bake them thoroughly." They used brick instead of stone, and tar for mortar. Then they said, "Come, let us build ourselves a city, with a tower that reaches to the heavens, so that we may make a name for ourselves; otherwise, we will be scattered over the face of the earth. But the LORD came down to see the city and the tower the people were building, so the Lord scattered them from there over all the earth, and they stopped building the city. That is why it is called Babel- because there the Lord confused the language of the whole world. From there the Lord scattered them over the face of the whole earth."

The Babylonians lived around the time of Nimrod which is after the flood and the days of Noah and in early Egyptian and late Sumerian history.

The tower of Babel was a center where all peoples would come to the land of Shinar to build this tower. From there they were scattered all over while also taking with them these Babylonian gods.

This is where many different cultures adopted the many gods of Babylon and took with them these idols, whereby, they renamed them in their own culture and language.

This is where the many gods of Egypt come from, and later in Greece and Rome, become the Greek and Roman gods.

Now what are the practices of Babylon? They believed and worshipped many gods and Nimrod made himself as an object of worship. They worshipped the sun and the moon and stars as gods, and he made himself to be a personified version of the Sun god.

Here he is known as, Nimrod, and his wife, Semiramis who is the moon goddess. They have a son, who is Tammuz, and later known as Baal or Moloch, known as the Canaanite god.

They sacrificed to these idol gods and had festivals and feast for these idols in the form of celebrations and rituals, which later became pagan or Babylonian holidays.

These were some of the names of the false idol gods of Babylon and these false deities who also come from Sumer. Names like An, Enlil, Enki, which are personifications of the sun, moon, and stars.

This pantheon of gods is known as, the Mesopotamian gods, who were shared between the Sumerians, the

Akkadians, and Babylonians. Many of the Sumerian gods were transferred over to Babylonian gods and their names were changed.

For example, Utu becomes Shamash, Inanna becomes Ishtar, Enki becomes Ea. These same pantheons of gods can be seen in Egyptian culture in the forms of Osiris and Isis and all their many false gods. All the way to ancient Greece and Rome in the forms of Zeus and Aphrodite and all their many false gods.

In Greece and Rome, we start to see more planetary gods, like the god of Jupiter, the Saturn god, and Venus goddess, and that these go beyond the sun and the moon. They begin to take from Egypt and Babylon the mystery school teachings and the worship of false idols.

Hermes shared the mystery school teachings of Egypt with Greek scholars and they began to form their own Greek mythology. They sculpt large stone statues of Zeus and Apollo and other false idols. They adopted the many false gods of Babylon and Egypt along with its practices and is why we so much similarity between these ancient mythologies.

From Greek mythology came Roman mythology. The Romans adopted the practices of the Greeks and mixed them with Germanic pagan gods and came up with their own false idols. The Romans named their gods after Germanic and Greek gods and associated them with the days of the week and the seven planets.

For example, Sunday is the Sun god, Monday the moon, Wednesday is Odin's day, Thursday is Thor's day, Friday is Freya's day, and Saturday is Saturn's day. This is how the romans made their weekly calendar in honor to their gods. They combined pagan gods with ancient gods and cosmology, making sure each has their day. We know that the One True God Created the heaven and the earth and rested in seven days. They try to worship their idols each of these days with festivals and sacrifices and to take away the true worship from God.

They wanted to be like God and have their own creation story, which gave birth to all their false idol gods like Zeus, Medusa, Hercules, and many others. No matter what form they take in culture they are the same fallen angels and false idol gods of old ancient civilizations that were to be washed away with the flood.

These false idol gods led to false idol worship, which led to false worship or false religion. These idols usually come with a doctrine or some type of practice or worship.

When studying these ancient cultures, we can see they practiced things like magic, rituals, and the worship of the sun and moon. With these practices and rituals, it gives birth to pagan religion and forms of worship.

From these forms of worship comes doctrines to support these beliefs and practices. These are where the stories or myths are created to support these beliefs. Mythology created a false doctrine that leaked and spread over into all philosophies and pagan religions.

The knowledge that was received on Mt. Hermon is the source of these doctrines. Let me explain, the emerald tablets of Thoth which are the mystery school teachings were adopted by Sumerians and Egyptians. The Egyptian mystery school teachings were adopted by the Greeks. The Greek mystery school teachings gave birth to philosophy and doctrines. This is where false doctrine and false religion come in the form of false worship.

The knowledge received by Hermes or Thoth was known as, Hermetics. This forbidden knowledge which was taught by fallen angels, teaches magic, sorcery, abominations, and idol worship. These practices are filled with abominations and blasphemies, that God does not like.

This knowledge teaches that evil is good, dark is light, and lucifer is god. Remember, Lucifer is the fallen angel who disguises himself as an angel of light and is the great deceiver and father of lies.

They worshipped these shining ones who came down on Mt. Hermon. This mystery knowledge was taken to Egypt and Thoth taught the mystery schools in Egypt, which is Kemetism.

King Solomon adopted this forbidden knowledge and practiced magic and sorcery, which he was not to do. This became known in Jewish practice, as the Kaballah.

The Kaballah doctrine and Hermeticism was then adopted by Greek philosophers, in which, they created the doctrine of Gnosticism.

These are what you call mystery school teachings and how they spread from Hermetics to Gnosticism, which is known as Esoteric. The esoteric or gnostic teachings are like Egyptian Kemetics and the Jewish Kaballah.

These practices and secret knowledge are normally practiced by secret societies. The free masons where the ones to invade Solomon's Temple, in which, they found the secret knowledge of Solomon. Free masons adopted the mystery school teachings of Egypt through Solomon's temple.

This created the illuminati and the secret societies. All this secret or forbidden knowledge comes from the fallen angels on Mt. Hermon who desired to be worshipped as gods and who give knowledge of the light bearer, or the one disguised as an angel of light, who is Lucifer.

The definition of Hermeticism according to Wikipedia states, *"Hermeticism, also called Hermetism, is a religious, philosophical, and esoteric tradition based primarily upon writings attributed to Hermes Trismegistus. These writings have greatly influenced the Western esoteric tradition. Kemetism is defined as, "Kemetism, also sometimes referred as Neterism, or Egyptian Neopaganism, is a revival of Ancient Egyptian religion and related expressions of religion in classical and late antiquity. Followers of Kemetism generally worship a few gods: Maat, Bast, Anubis, Sekhmet or Thoth, among others, but recognize* the existence of every god. This worship generally takes the form of prayer and setting up altars, but there are no set guidelines for worship. Altars can contain items such as candles, offerings, or statues." Kabbalah is defined as, "An esoteric method, discipline, and school of thought in Jewish mysticism." The definition of Gnosticism is, "A collection of ancient religious ideas and systems which originated in the first century A.D among early Christians and Jewish sects. These various groups emphasized personal spiritual knowledge (gnosis) over orthodox teachings, traditions, and ecclesiastical authority. Gnostic cosmogony generally presents a distinction between a supreme, hidden God and a malevolent lesser divinity responsible for creating the material universe. Viewing this material existence as flawed or evil, Gnostics considered the principal element of salvation to be direct knowledge of the supreme divinity in the form of mystical or esoteric insight. Many Gnostic texts deal not in concepts of sin and repentance, but with illusion and enlightenment."

Source states that, "False doctrine is any teaching that distorts, is contrary to, adds to, or takes away from what is taught in the Bible. Sound doctrine is teaching found in and consistent with what is taught in the Bible. Doctrine in its simplest form is a teaching. The Bible describes doctrines of man, doctrines of demons, and doctrines of God. Discernment is the practice of determining whether what is being taught is a true teaching or a false one.

When studying these ancient religions and ancient philosophies we begin to see they are filled with idols, magic, and secret knowledge. We know the source of all this knowledge was received on Mt. Hermon through the fallen angels and lucifer.

These mystical and mythological beliefs turned into philosophical concepts and ideologies. These philosophies which are teachings are considered doctrines. When you take a deep look into each of these doctrines, we see they do not line up with the Word of God and in most cases go directly against it.

These false doctrines lead to false teachings, false prophets, and false worship. Most of the time leading to worship of idols, worship of self, or worship of evil. What makes these doctrines false is that they twist the truth and present their own ideas to replace the truth.

These doctrines teach things like, there is no God or Devil, that good and evil are only ideas, that you are God, that darkness is light, they blaspheme God and Christ, and practice magic and sorcery.

This is the knowledge that they carry that has been passed on over time since the fallen angels and lucifer. A knowledge that teaches that evil is good, darkness is light, and that lucifer is god. This is false idol worship and false doctrine of luciferianism. Our battle is not with people or demons but with false doctrine, which are the "schemes of the devil."

Isiah 5:20 "Woe to those who call evil good and good evil, who put darkness for light and light for darkness, who put bitter for sweet and sweet for bitter!

Deuteronomy 18:10 "Let no one be found among you who sacrifices their son or daughter in the fire, who practices divination or sorcery, interprets omens, or engages in witchcraft."

2 Corinthians 11:14 "No wonder, for even Satan disguises himself as an angel of light."

Ephesians 6:11 "Put on the full armor of God, so that you will be able to stand firm against the schemes of the devil.

This forbidden knowledge or secret knowledge that was received by Hermes became known as, Hermetics. This knowledge was shared with the Greeks and became known as, Gnosticism. Solomon adopted this Hermetics and it became known as, the Kaballah. The Masons invaded Solomon's Temple and received this mystery knowledge which became known as, Free Masonry or Secret Societies.

The Free Masons created another doctrine which became known as, the illuminati or the enlightened ones. In this doctrine they teach a secret knowledge that claims lucifer is god. This all leads up to luciferianism, which is the worship of lucifer, or the illuminated one. All roads come from Babylon on Mt. Hermon and all roads lead to luciferianism.

In Conclusion, we see that lucifer was an angel who rebelled against God, in which, he was cast out of heaven. Lucifer, also known as Satan, who is the adversary of God, caused a third of the angels to fall with him.

These fallen angels are recorded to have come down on Mt. Hermon where ancient civilizations seen them as light beings or gods. They received secret or forbidden knowledge from these fallen angels and where taught things like magic, sorcery, and idolatry.

Hermes Trismegistus recorded this knowledge in the emerald tablets of Thoth. Hermes was in the time of the Sumerians and traveled to Egypt to share Hermeticism. This is where he taught the mystery school teachings of Egypt which led to Kemetism.

Solomon adopted this mystery school teaching of magic and rituals and this led to the Kabbalah. Along with all these practices, pagan religions, and doctrines were associated with idols and rituals.

The Greeks then adopt this doctrine in the form of Gnosticism, in which, gives philosophical views to mythological concepts. We see that from Sumer, Egypt, Greece, and Rome they were all filled with pagan idol worship and rituals that are ancient in origin.

This false idol worship led to false doctrines, practices, and beliefs, contrary to the bible. We see the devil has schemes to deceive and confuse those from the truth and desires to twist the truth with false doctrines.

These doctrines and philosophies are adopted by secret societies and free masons. The free masons teach about enlightenment which are concepts from Gnosticism and about illumination which are concepts of the illuminati.

This doctrine teaches that the enlightened one will become illuminated with truth, which is, that darkness is light, evil is good, and lucifer is god. This on the contrary is not the truth but in total opposition to the truth. It is a false doctrine and is a lie.

John 8:44 "You are of your father the devil, and you want to do the desires of your father. He was a murderer from the beginning and does not stand in the truth because there is no truth in him. Whenever he speaks a lie, he speaks from his own nature, for he is a liar and the father of lies."

In retrospect, we can see described in the bible, the One and Only True God had dealt with the gods of Egypt and showed His supreme power and Sovereignty over their false gods and destroyed them. We also see that the One and Only True God also dealt with Babylon and Nimrod and the gods of Babylon, whereby, once again He displays His true power over their false gods and destroys them.

Each time from Egypt to Babylon we see that God sets his people free from their idolatry and warns them to leave them behind. We see that God had dealt with the gods of Egypt, the Babylonian gods, and Roman gods, in that, they were all destroyed.

Egypt was left in ruins, Babylon no longer exist, and Rome has fallen. Satan and these fallen angels have caused men to worship them in the form of idols made of stone and wood. Therefore, The One True God destroyed their idols so that all will know, that there is Only One True God and that He rightfully deserves worship for He is our Creator.

The One True God who Created the Heavens and the Earth and all things in it, who Created the sun, moon, and stars, and rested in seven days. The One True God who is a Spirit and He desires that we worship Him in Spirit and in Truth.

He does not want us bowing down to things made by hand, things of wood and stone, but to worship Him in Spirit. So that we do not worship the creation but that we worship the Creator. God is Sovereign over all creation and rightfully deserves our thanks, praise, and worship. This is true worship in Spirit and in Truth.

Chapter 12

Eternal Life After Death

Is there life after death? Is there a life after this life? The Bible speaks of a first death and a second death which alludes to the fact that there is a second life. When it says in the Bible "in this life and the life to come" this alludes to the idea that there is a life after this life.

This must be true because Christ speaks of eternal life and if it were not true, Christ would not have said so. Christ mentioning everlasting life numerous times gives assurance that there is an everlasting eternal life that comes after this temporary life.

You must wonder where do we go when we die? Is there life after this life? Some say the dead are resting in peace, some say the dead know nothing, some say the dead are in heaven. When does this next life start? Is it instant in the twinkling of an eye, is it at the end of this life, or is it at the second coming of Christ?

Is the coming of Christ both when a person passes away from this world and an ultimate end of all things? I believe once a person passes away, they are met with Christ and taken away into Paradise, which is the next life or the afterlife and which is eternal life. I believe the body is at rest or is dead in the grave having no thought and the spirit leaves the body to go be with the Lord.

Where He is so will we be. To be absent from the body is to be in the presence of the Lord. Christ tells us that He goes to prepare a place for us, that His Father's mansion has many rooms, which this place is Paradise.

He tells the thief on the cross, "this day you will be with me in Paradise." If this is so, then that day when the thief died on the cross, although his body laid to rest, Christ said he will be with him in Paradise. This is the place that Christ has prepared for us. This place is heaven or paradise, and this is where we go when we die.

When Christ returns in the Second Coming, He will resurrect the dead and those spirits in heaven will receive their new bodies, after this the believers who are alive on the earth will pass from death and instantly be transformed into the new spiritual body.

Christ says that His kingdom is not of this world, meaning not like this physical world, and that no flesh or blood can enter the kingdom of God. This means that only the spirit can enter the kingdom.

So, that also means the kingdom is not of this world and is spiritual, we also know from Corinthians that the spiritual comes after the natural, the imperishable after the perishable, and the eternal after the temporary. Christ is saying that the kingdom will come after this world, after this life, after the natural and that we will be where He is in heaven.

The kingdom is heaven, paradise, and eternal life. To enter the kingdom, you would have to be out the flesh, which means to be absent from the body, which means after death. This also means that there is life after death and the next life or life to come is eternal life in heaven.

This is the kingdom that is not of this world, a place that was prepared for us. Think what does it mean to have something prepared for? Prepared for what? I would say a place prepared for us for when we die and pass away from this world. A place that was prepared for us since the beginning and is being restored in Christ.

I will look at some scriptures that speak about the kingdom of heaven, eternal life, and paradise.

John 14:3 "And if I go and prepare a place for you, I will come back and take you to be with me that you also may be where I am."

John 14:2 "My Father's house has many rooms; if that were not so, would I have told you that I am going there to prepare a place for you?"

John 14:4 "You know the way to the place where I am going." Thomas said to him, 'Lord, we don't know where you are going, so how can we know the way?" Jesus answered, "I am the way and the truth and the life. No one comes to the Father except through me."

John 20:17 "Jesus said, "Do not hold on to me, for I have not yet ascended to the Father. Go instead to my brother and tell them, 'I am ascending to my Father and your Father, to my God and your God."

Here we see Christ mentioning that He is going to His Father's house which is heaven and He goes to prepare a place for us. If it were not so, He would not have said so. We know the place which where He is going. Jesus explains that He is the way to heaven, the truth, and the way to eternal life.

It is through Christ that we go to God our Father, in which, Christ goes to prepare a place for us and will come to get us to be where He is. He says, "My Father's house has many rooms like a mansion." This mansion of many rooms must be the Kingdom of God and Heaven.

This is where Christ says I go and prepare a place for you. Where I will be you will be there with me, and I will come back to get you. After death where do you think you go? It is a spiritual place for His kingdom is not of this world. Heaven is a dwelling place. It is also a state of mind and state of being. It is also a place we go in the end when we die. It is what comes after the natural, it is the spiritual world.

We know Christ dwells in the highest heavens and sits at the right hand of God. This is the dwelling place He speaks of when He says, "I am going to my God and your God." This place is where Christ comes and takes us away to. This could be at our death or at the second coming. This could be the resurrection or paradise until the resurrection.

Here are some scriptures from 1 Corinthians 15 that explains the natural man and the spiritual man. Showing how the natural comes first then the spiritual.

1 Corinthians 15:47 The first man was of the dust of the earth; the second man is of heaven. 48 As was the earthly man, so are those who are of the earth; and as is the heavenly man, so also are those who are of heaven. 49 And just as we have borne the image of the earthly man, so shall we bear the image of the heavenly man. - Just as we are now like the earthly man, we will someday be like the heavenly man. 50 I declare to you, brothers and sisters, that flesh and blood cannot inherit the kingdom of God, nor does the perishable inherit the imperishable. 51 Listen, I tell you a mystery: We will not all die, but we will all be transformed. 52 in a flash, in the twinkling of an eye, at the last trumpet. For the trumpet will sound, the dead will be raised imperishable, and we will all be changed. 53 For the perishable must clothe itself with the imperishable, and the mortal with immortality. For our dying bodies must be transformed into bodies that will never die; our mortal bodies must be transformed into immortal bodies. 54 When the perishable has been clothed with the imperishable, and the mortal with immortality, then the saying that is written will come true: "Death has been swallowed up in victory." 55 "Where, O death, is your victory? Where, O death, is your sting?" 56 The sting of death is sin, and the power of sin is the law. 57 But thanks be to God! He gives us the victory through our Lord Jesus Christ.

This scripture explains how the natural man or earthly man who is of the dust of the earth is the first man and the spiritual man or heavenly man who is of heaven comes second.

The earthly man is flesh and blood and is perishable and mortal. The spiritual man who is of spirit is imperishable and immortal. Just as we bear the image of the earthly man, we shall also bear the image of the heavenly man.

Christ explains that flesh and blood cannot enter the kingdom and that we all must be changed and transformed. That not all will die but be transformed at death or the last trumpet. This is when the saying will be true "Death has been swallowed up in victory" because we have victory over death through Christ by God. That death has no power and is defeated by Christ because we have been transformed into the eternal spiritual body.

Hebrews 9:27 Just as each person is destined to die once and after that comes judgment, 28 so Christ was sacrificed once to take away the sins of many; and he will appear a second time, not to bear sin, but to bring salvation to those who are waiting for him.

Luke 18:29 "Truly I tell you, "Jesus said to them, "no one who has given up house or wife or brothers or parents or children, for the sake of the Kingdom of God, 30 who will be repaid many times over in this life, and will have eternal life in the world to come." - "Truly, truly, I say to you, he who hears my word, and believes Him who sent me, has eternal life, and does not come into judgement, but has passed out of death into life."

John 3:16 "For God so loved the world, that He gave His only begotten Son, that whoever believes in Him shall not perish, but have eternal life."

Here we see that each person is destined to die once and after that comes judgement. That Christ came the first time for sacrifice and to take away the sins of the world and that He will appear a second time to bring salvation to those who are waiting for Him.

Anyone who has given up their life for God and for the sake of the Kingdom will be repaid in this life and the life to come with eternal life. That whoever believes in Christ and the One who sent Him will pass from death to life and does not come into judgement.

That God loved us so much that He gave His only Son for us so that we may not perish but have eternal life. It is wonderful to know that God did not abandon nor forsake us but forgave us and saved us from death.

I look at this and ask the question, when does judgment or resurrection occur? Is it at the end of one's life or at the second coming of Christ and the last trumpet? Is the second coming at the end of this life where Christ returns and takes us away to where He is? And is the last trumpet the day each person dies?

It says that each person lives and is destined to die then face judgement, but those who believe in Christ will not come into judgement and will pass over to eternal life. Does this all occur when you pass away from this earth or at the end of the world?

We know that this must take place after death, but does it all happen at once and the dead are sleeping now, or does it happen at each person's passing? I will investigate this further, but I believe that when we die, we are judged or pass from judgement to life. If you are judged, it will be the separation of the sheep from the goats. This judgement I believe occurs when you die and that Christ also returns to us and saves us from death, bringing us to the place where He is, which is Heaven.

I also believe in the actual Second Coming of Christ when He returns to the earth all the spirits in heaven will be resurrected into their new spiritual bodies and the ones on the earth will be instantly transformed and we together will have received our new eternal bodies at the last trumpet.

When does this occur? Well let's look at the story of the thief on the cross. This scripture reads as, Luke 23:39-43 *"Then one of the criminals who were hanged blasphemed Him, saying, "If you are the Christ, save yourself and us."*

But the other, answering, rebuked him, saying, "Do you not even fear God, seeing you are under the same condemnation? And we indeed justly, for we receive the due reward of our deeds; but this Man has done nothing wrong." Then he said to Jesus, "Lord, remember me when you come into your kingdom." And Jesus said to him, "Assuredly, I say to you, today you will be with Me in Paradise."

Here we can see that the thief on the cross understood that we all are under condemnation and that each man receives his due reward for our deeds. But Christ who is without sin had done no wrong. The thief asked Christ for forgiveness and asked that Christ remember him when He comes into His kingdom.

Christ answers him saying, "Assuredly, I say to you, "today" you will be with me in Paradise. We can see that Christ says to him in assurance that today he will be with him in Paradise. This means Christ is already coming into the kingdom and that today is the day. This means that when the thief died on the cross, although his bodied laid to rest, he went to go be with the Lord that day.

This alludes to the idea that these things occur after death and the second coming can well be at the day of our death, which is also like the twinkling of an eye. That as you die and you instantly are transformed and are received by Christ and taken away into Paradise.

Also, the second coming will be at the end of ages and the believers who are alive will also be transformed instantly, in the twinkling of an eye, and receive their new eternal bodies, passing from death to life, and being reunited with the dead in Christ.

At this moment, scripture says that death is swallowed up for all the believer's dead and alive have all been transformed. The dead in Christ are resurrected to their new bodies returning with Christ from Heaven and the alive in Christ that are resurrected when Christ returns.

Sources from a Wikipedia reference write about Eternal life and explain everlasting life, resurrection of the body, and the second coming. Let's look.

Eternal life traditionally refers to continued life after death, as outlined in Christian eschatology. The Apostles' Creed testifies; "I believe... the resurrection of the body, and life everlasting." In this view, eternal life commences after the second coming of Jesus and the resurrection of the dead, although in the New Testament's Johannine literature there are references to eternal life commencing in the earthly life of the believer, possibly indicating an inaugurated eschatology.

According to mainstream Christian theology, after death but before the second coming, the saved live with God in an intermediate state, but after the Second Coming, they experience the physical resurrection of the dead and the physical recreation of a New Earth.

The Catechism of the Catholic Church states, "By death the soul is separated from the body, but in the resurrection, God will give incorruptible life to our body, transformed by reunion with our soul. Just as Christ is risen and lives forever, so all of us will rise at the last day." Wright argues that "God's plan is not to abandon this world... Rather, he intends to remake it. And when He does, he will raise all people to new bodily life to live in it. That is the promise of the Christian gospel.

2 Corinthians 5:9 "So we make it our aim to please him, whether we are at home in the body or away from it. 10 For we must all appear before the judgement seat of Christ, so that each one may receive what is due for what he has done in the body, whether good or evil."

1 Thessalonians 4:15 "According to the Lord's word, we tell you that we who are still alive, who are left until the coming of the Lord, will certainly not precede those who have fallen asleep. 16 For the Lord himself will come down from heaven, with a loud command, with the voice of the archangel and with the trumpet call of God, and the dead in Christ will rise first. 17 After that, we who are still alive and are left will be caught up together with them in the clouds to meet the Lord in the air. And so, we will be with the Lord forever."

This is the second coming of Christ but when does this occur? According to the Lord those who are alive will not precede those who have fallen asleep. That the dead in Christ will rise first then those who are alive at the second coming.

The ones who are alive at the time of Christ return will be transformed and meet with Christ in the air. We know that after death we must appear before the judgement seat of Christ and receive our due reward. This reward is heaven and eternal life. This either happens at death or at the second coming, so this creates two scenarios.

One scenario is that we face judgement after death and go to heaven and then return to the earth when Christ returns. The other scenario is we rest in peace after death and are in the grave until the second coming of Christ and then are resurrected to life and go to heaven. Let's look at both scenarios.

In the first scenario, when someone dies, they are in the grave resting in peace, they know nothing or can do nothing. They are in the grave until Christ returns then they are resurrected and go to heaven together with the people who are alive.

Or the second scenario, when someone dies, they face judgement and go to heaven then return to earth with Christ when He returns in the Second Coming. They then receive their new bodies along with the ones who are alive.

One scenario creates the image that when people die, they are in the grave and await judgement and the resurrection until Christ returns. The other creates an image that when people die, they face judgement and receive their due reward or punishment. They go to heaven and await the resurrection of the body in Christ's return.

One says you die and wait to go to heaven. The other says you die and go to be with the Lord in heaven until you return to earth with Christ and meet with those who are alive.

Some believe the dead are in the grave and know nothing, some others believe that the dead are in heaven and watch over them. Some believe you die and rest in peace, some others believe you die and go to be with the Lord.

I believe that the when a person dies the body is at rest in the grave, but the spirit goes to be with the Lord in heaven. I believe that when someone dies, they are transformed into the Spirit and go to be judged, there they receive their reward and go to heaven.

This is where the dead in Christ go. They are alive in heaven and await the return of Christ. The dead in Christ will return to the earth with Christ when He returns to restore the New earth. Then we will receive our new eternal bodies along together with the ones who are resurrected.

In the first scenario if the dead are in the grave then how can they come with Christ when he returns? They come with Christ when he returns because they are in Heaven with Him, not in the grave. Their bodies are laid to rest in the grave and they will return in the future coming of Christ to receive their newly resurrected bodies.

The ones who are alive at the time of Christ's coming will then be transformed and instantly pass from death to life and receive their newly resurrected bodies. Together we are gathered together on the new heaven and new earth.

There is this life and the life to come, this life and the afterlife, the natural and the spiritual, the temporary and the eternal, the perishable and the imperishable, and the mortal who must put on immortality.

First comes the natural then comes the spiritual. After this natural life comes eternal life in the spiritual through Christ Jesus, from our Father, who is the source of all life.

For there is life in the Father so as there is life in the Son. He did not abandon nor forsake us, but He loved us and saved us. He saved us from sin and death, Christ died for our sins and gives us Eternal life after death.

In Conclusion, we are born in the flesh as the natural man and through death we are reborn in Christ as the spiritual man. For the first man was Adam and the second man Christ.

We all are born in this life and wait for the life to come. We live we die then we live eternally. Some of us may not die but be transformed at the Second Coming of Christ.

That we all must be transformed both the dead and the alive in Christ so the saying holds true and scripture is fulfilled, when it says "Death is swallowed up", "Hades where is your victory", "O Death where is your sting."

For Christ has the keys to Hades and Death. For he destroys death and the grave. For through him we are resurrected and have eternal life. That he has prepared a place for us when we die and that we will be where He is, which is heaven or paradise.

That every man is destined to die once and then judgment. Then you receive your reward in heaven until the Day of Resurrection. When they will return with Christ to receive their new bodies.

If we are alive at the time of Christ's coming then we will pass from death to life and instantly be transformed into the new eternal body. This is the eternal life that God promised through His Son.

That through him we have life more abundantly, which is eternal life after death.

Remember the scripture that says, unless it dies first. Then it is raised up incorruptible, in strength, honor, and glory, where the mortal puts on immortality and the perishable is clothed with the imperishable.

That even though we die we live. For Christ says anyone who is in me although they may die, they live.

John 11:25 "Jesus said to her, "I am the resurrection and the life. He who believes in Me, though he may die, he shall live."

John 8:24 "I told you that you would die in your sins; if you do not believe that I am he, you will indeed die in your sins."

John 11:26 "And whoever lives and believes in Me shall never die. Do you believe this?"

John 5:24 "Truly, truly, I say to you, whoever hears my word and believes him who sent me has eternal life. He does not come into judgment, but has passed from death to life."

John 1:12 "Yet to all who did receive him, to those who believed in his name, he gave the right to become children of God"

1 Peter 1:23 "Those who have been born again are born "not of perishable seed, but of imperishable, through the living and enduring word of God."

Colossians 3:24 "knowing that from the Lord you will receive the inheritance as your reward. You are serving the Lord Christ."

1 Peter 1:4 "to an inheritance that can never perish, spoil, or fade. This inheritance is kept in heaven for you."

Romans 6:23 "For the wages of sin is death, but the gift of God is eternal life in Christ Jesus our Lord."

Conclusion

In Conclusion, I hope we were able to gain the deeper truths and understandings of the Bible. To be firm in the word and grounded and rooted in faith that produces good fruit.

Understanding who God is, who His Son is, and who the Holy Spirit is. Understanding that there is one God the Father and there is no other God besides Him. That He shares a relationship with His Son and that the Holy Spirit makes them one.

Understanding that God is Good and stands for what is right. That He is Good, He is Love, and He is Light. That He is oneness in a world full of duality.

Understanding that we must discern and choose between good and evil, life and death, and that we either become sheep or goats, wheat or tares, or the good tree or the bad tree.

Understanding that the flesh wars against the Spirit and that there is a battle between good and evil. A battle between the Spirit and the flesh and a battle between principalities of darkness in high places.

Understanding that we are baptized by water for proclaiming our faith in Jesus Christ and the forgiveness of sins, and that we are baptized by the Holy Spirit which refines and purifies us. That water baptism is a sign of one's faith and the spirit baptism the sealing of the Holy Spirit. That we must be born again of water and of spirit.

That God's law is to love, and that love fulfills the law. Understanding the difference between law and grace, self-righteous works and the righteousness of God. The difference between works and faith, and that we produce good fruit in good faith through the Spirit.

That works and faith are proportional to each other in a contrasted complementary fashion but are being used together in a tandem order, with faith being first. That faith without works is dead and works without faith is dead, however, faith and works work together, in which, faith alone saves that produces good fruit is a true faith that is proven by its fruit.

Understanding that the spiritual comes after the natural, the imperishable after the perishable, and the butterfly comes after the caterpillar. That there is this life and the life to come. The eternal life given through the Holy Spirit by Jesus Christ. For as there is life in the Father so there is also eternal life in the Son.

That we are His Sheep and that where He will be, we will also be. That there is heaven or paradise that is prepared for us. That God did not abandon us nor forsake us, but He loved us, forgave us, and saved us through His Son.

His Word keeps us rooted and grounded in love and faith and helps us to stand firm on His Word and to be firm in goodness and truth, in that, it produces strong branches which is faith that produces good fruit.

To know that Christ is the vine and God is the gardener. That if we remain in Him and He remain in us, that we will produce good fruit. That outside of Him we can do nothing. That God prunes us and cultivates us, feeding us through His Word and sustaining us through faith.

I hope this reading has revealed a deeper truth and understanding of the Bible. That a good seed is planted in good soil and that it reaps a hundred-fold. That God cultivates the ground and waters it with His word that it grows strong roots of faith and produce good fruit.

———————

Copyright © 2020 Michael J Hnatowicz III

All rights reserved. No part of this publication may be reproduced, distributed, or transmitted in any form or by any means, including photocopying, recordings, or other electronic or mechanical methods, without the prior written consent of the publisher, except in the case of brief quotations embodied in critical reviews and certain other noncommercial uses permitted by copyright law. For permission requests, write to the publisher, addressed "Attentions: Permissions Coordinator," at the address below.

ISBN: 978-1-7376810-0-7 (Paperback)

ISBN: 978-1-7376810-2-1 (Electronic book)

Any references to historical events, real people, or real places are used fictitiously. Names, characters, and places are products of the authors imagination.

Book Design by Michael J Hnatowicz III

First Printing Edition, 2022

Meek Music and Publishing LLC

300 Colonial Center Parkway STE 100N
Roswell GA 30076

www.ingramcontent.com/pod-product-compliance
Lightning Source LLC
Chambersburg PA
CBHW050413120526
44590CB00015B/1942